asian style hotels

BALI   JAVA   MALAYSIA   SINGAPORE   THAILAND

Kim Inglis

photography by
Jacob Termansen and Pia Marie Molbech

PERIPLUS

contents

The New Asian Hotel

Southeast Asia has long been renowned for its hospitality industry. Home to some stunning hotels, where exceptionally high standards of service, glorious architecture and gorgeous surrounds combine with clement weather, it has consistently lured sun-seekers and culture vultures in equal measure. With a plethora of Nirvana-like packages, its hotels have been soothing tired souls and rejuvenating the world weary for decades — all the while injecting a little Eastern magic into the experience.

A beach in Bali? A retreat in the hills in Thailand? A volcano-clad Javan hillside home? A city-state hub? There are locations and styles to tantalize every traveler. Some have utilized vernacular building traditions and materials in their design, while others have relied on the beauty and serenity of site. All, however, have harnessed the innate grace of the local populations. Showcasing their culture and traditions has been an integral part of the package. After all, a gentle oriental smile that lights up the whole face goes a long way towards guest satisfaction.

Today, however, customers are demanding a bit more than a sweet smile. They want greater sophistication, better facilities, more entertainment. As a result, adding to the tried-and-tested brands, there is now a host of new hotels. Thrusting upstarts, they're tech savvy, cutting-edge design wise, snappy on the service, and more often than not intelligent and stylish too. Architecturally, some are very modern — think stark, cubist white boxes set against a glittering blue sea for example — while others appear more traditional, heavily disguising flat plasma tv screens, wireless internet access and other mod-cons behind a veneer of the vernacular. Whatever the style, however, the message is clear.

We are in a new world where the standards of the past are simply that. In the past. Nowadays, highly mobile travelers want all the conveniences of home and office when they are on holiday. In addition, they require drop-dead design, generous room sizes, personalized service, high-tech TV, internet and DVD systems, and plenty of choice — in activities, spas, cuisines, entertainment and more. The region is responding.

For the most part, it's these new kids on the block we feature in this book, though of course we don't neglect some of the older, top-end hotels too. Each has been selected for its sense of individuality and style, as well as its facilities and service. Be it a louche metropolitan oasis, a villa on the beach or a hangout in the hills — it has been designed with you in mind. Enjoy.

The Balé Nusa Dua

Originally intended as an island retreat for its three Jakarta-based owners, the Balé occupies a hilly rise on Bali's Jimbaran peninsula enclave. Holding a maximum of 40 guests in 17 private villas, many with ocean views to the east, it is an adult-only retreat. A rigorous, stylish haven for those in search of seclusion, the Balé opened in December 2001. Modernist, minimal, serene and exclusive, it quickly gained membership to the Small Luxury Hotels of the World group — and its international reputation was assured.

"At the Balé we want our guests to feel at home rather than in a resort," says the youthful general manager, Jose Luis Calle, "We want them to relax and spend quality time with their partner; the idea is to pamper them with personalized service, custom-made meals, spa treatments or programs and, above all, friendly and discreet service." This they undoubtedly get — and in a setting that throws conventional Bali style out with the bathwater. Certainly, this is made-in-Bali, glazed-in-Bali and carved-in-Bali, but it is more Zen den than trad Balinese *balé*.

Architect Antony Liu (with partner Ferry Ridwan) maintains a restrained palette throughout. A clean, pared-back look stretches across the compact 1.1-hectare (2.5-acre) plot. Outside, walls combine smooth *paras* Jogja stone with rough local limestone; landscaping by Karl Princic is of the rushes, reeds and cactus school; and simple cascading water and grey pebbles are used to cool what is clearly quite a hot site. Inside, villas are steadfastly monochrome, as is the lobby where the longest reception desk I've ever seen is punctured only by a single computer and one member of staff dressed in white.

Also oversized are the villas — and everything in them. The bed, raised on a terrazzo plinth, is huge; custom-carved cabinetry in dark *merbau* wood is solidly

imposing. The television screen is 29 inch (73 cm) wide. Even the private plunge pool is less plunge, more pool. The adjacent cushioned *balé* seats six comfortably. Surfaces are unadorned, with a gold mesh panel above the bed the only decorative element. Bathrooms feature indoor and outdoor showers, twin vanities as well as an hourglass-shaped tub.

If all this sounds slightly puritanical, it isn't. Feminine touches, such as an aromatic selection of hand-made soaps and a floating flower and candle arrangement in the bathroom, humanize the villas. A bevy of butlers are on call, but if you fancy a snack, a jar of home-baked cookies is thoughtfully provided. Staff, 90 percent of whom are Balinese with 85 percent picked from the local *banjar* or village, are genuinely enthusiastic. A great selection of novels, magazines, and video and music CDs are available on request.

Children under 16 are banned from the Balé. This makes sense here and forms part of the ongoing commitment of management company Sanctuary Resorts in providing opportunities for guests to balance body, mind and spirit. The spa is a haven for the senses, and visiting yoga, Shiatsu and other alternative healers and practitioners make up a regular round robin of Masters in Residence. These, along with the adult-only policy, the sophisticated serenity of the site and absolute privacy, encourage guests to de-stress and rejuvenate.

Because each individual villa is set in its own walled enclosure, a high proportion of guests remain ensconced in their rooms for the duration of their stay. The heat of the day encourages villa siesta-seekers and spa-goers; even the main pool is often eschewed in favor of a quiet nap or a serious snooze plunge poolside. However, you may spot the odd couple beneath an umbrella, or at the hotel's aptly named restaurant, Faces. Here, light French food influenced with Asian flavors and organic produce form the dishes of the day. However, this is not a resort where guests go to meet and mingle. You may discover a few things about yourself, but you're unlikely to discover a new best friend.

Tempted? If a serious chill-out is in order, an anniversary with a loved one is coming up or you want to do some contemplative body/mind work, the Balé may be just the ticket. And as Calle says: "When we say goodbye to guests who after a few days look younger, more relaxed and positive, it means we must be doing something right." Hear hear.

Jalan Raya Kusa Dua Selatan, PO Box 76,
Nusa Dua, Bali 80363, Indonesia.
tel: +62 361 775 111   fax: +62 361 775 222
bliss@thebalé.com   www.sanctuaryresorts.com

Downtown Villas Seminyak

Seminyak is to Bali what San Antonio is to Ibiza — the hippest part of the island. It's where cool young things congregate to club, shop, chill and catch up. Appropriate, then, that it houses Bali's hottest hotel — a series of modish residences called Downtown Villas.

The usual combo of rice paddy views, thatched pavilions and *gamelan* music is eschewed at Downtown for something unashamedly urban in concept and context. "The idea for Downtown (yes, downtown Seminyak)," explains one of the youthful co-owners Guy Neale, "was to move away from the open villa with traditional *alang-alang* to something more contemporary and comfortable. We felt the time was right to give discerning visitors an alternative style of accommodation with the kind of functionality they expect elsewhere in the world."

Neale clearly had his finger on the tourist pulse, because Downtown proved a hit from the start. Offering nine one- to three-bedroom villas, reservations are more than recommended. They're obligatory.

Boat builder turned designer Fredo Taffin, who had previously designed hip eatery Ku de Ta (also owned by some of Downtown's partners) and a variety of Bali villas, was the architect of choice. His brief was to create "a downtown luxury hideaway with a contemporary feel" — and he obliged by combining a modern international ethos with Bali's rich natural materials. *Merbau* wood, teak, terrazzo, andesite stone, granite and grey soapstone are all used — but are married with slick finishing rather than traditional carving and fashioning.

All the villas have private kitchens, pools and some outside space, but all are individually designed with sleek, clean-lined furniture from Australian firm Urban Icon. The larger, two-story villas have a private 20-meter (66-foot) lap pool, wooden

sun deck with steel mesh loungers, and a contemporary take on the open-sided *balé*. Open kitchens are kitted out with Italian aluminum fittings, and sanitary ware is of the high-quality, imported variety. Leather and suede sofas, conceptual art pieces by Véronique Aonzo and brash color combos are more metropolitan than insular — yet work well in the Seminyak setting.

In many ways Downtown Villas is representative of a new wave of architectural experimentation that has swept across the island since the millennium. What long-term Bali resident architect Gianni Francione terms a "new tropical internationalism," it is characterized by a marriage of modernist forms, Western technical know-how and the innate adaptability and skills of the Balinese. The romance of the rustic is increasingly being replaced by a challenging cosmopolitanism. Homes and villas, restaurants, hotels and homestays are finding that a rice field view and a dash of island charm are limited commodities nowadays. People are demanding — and getting — more.

According to Neale, Downtown's mission is to give the international traveler an experience that only a modern apartment hotel can offer. There is no hotel restaurant, but a quick phone call will ensure delivery of dishes from the all day dining menu; these are cooked in the hotel kitchens. Alternatively, villa kitchens are stocked with basics, so you can make a cup of tea, coffee or a snack at any time of the day — but if you prefer, staff can man the stove and cook for you. This is ideal if you are in one of the larger villas, and feel like having a group dinner by the pool. You can also order food items from the market or supermarket if you feel like cooking yourself. Flexibility is key.

Even though Downtown is situated in the heart of Seminyak, it is located off a relatively traffic-free, quiet street. Inward looking, architecturally and conceptually, it is sequestered and secluded. In addition, the villas' understated modern design is soothing after the buzz of a club night or a shopping trawl down Jalan Raya Seminyak. Modern holidaymakers find they offer just the right ambience to come home to.

Jalan Lalu Village 9d, Seminyak, Bali 80361, Indonesia.
tel: +62 361 736 464   fax: +62 361 736 424
info@downtownbali.com   www.downtownbali.com

The Legian Seminyak

Jakarta-based designer Jaya Ibrahim began his career under the tutelage of designer and couturier Anouska Hempel. Today, she is rightly attributed as the creator of the first "designer hotel" — Blakes in London. Applauded for its startling originality at a time when homogeneity in hotel design was the norm, the design ethos at Blakes is flamboyant and sensual. It's interesting, therefore, that Ibrahim's first major project — the interior and furniture design at the Legian in Bali — is just the opposite: restrained, muted, cool, elegant.

While Blakes is dark, dusky and enigmatic, the Legian is open, airy and light. Naturally, this is partly due to site, climate and architecture, but it nonetheless marks a departure for Ibrahim and the development of his own highly individual style. Justly celebrated by the creative cognoscenti, the Legian marks a milestone in resort interiors. Over the ensuing decade, Ibrahim's work went on to make global design waves: Copies of his furniture designs may be seen in hotels as far afield as the US and Europe.

Even though it dates from 1993, the Legian retains a fresh, modern perspective in both public and private spaces. This is partly because of the calm interior design palette, and partly because of its stunning natural location. Fronting the ocean, and built very close (some suggest too close) to the shore, every part of the hotel is focused on the relentless energy coming from the sea.

"I wanted everybody to be drawn by the sea," explains Ibrahim, "that is what the Legian is all about. It isn't about the interior, or the food, or the design; it is about the power of the sea." Certainly when you are within the hotel precincts, it's difficult to take your eyes off the huge expanse of ocean and horizon. Everything faces toward it. Whether you are wallowing in the swimming pool where overflow

edge optically meets the waves, sitting on your suite's private balcony, or taking a meal in the restaurant, the sound and sight of surf is ever-present.

The Legian was the first hotel in Bali constructed in a completely contemporary building language. Indonesian architect Dedi Kusnadi made a deliberate break with vernacular architectural style (although there is a central tower in the style of a Balinese drum tower or *balé kul-kul*) for what was originally an apartment building. Once the decision was made to transform it into an all-suite hotel (all rooms have small pantries as well as bed-, bath- and living-rooms), the hotel retained this slightly urban air. It is built over four stories in a number of linked structures, all interconnected by covered walkways in ivory and biscuit-hued *paras* and limestone.

On arrival, the lobby sets the tone. An enormous carved screen by Balinese master carver I Made Jojol takes its inspiration from Walter Spies' paintings from the 1930s. Flanking it are two life-sized guardian statues carved from albasia, a balsa wood that is often used for traditional musical instruments. Their fluid shapes and beautiful grain are restful and tactile. Through the perforated screen you can see a carving of waves on the restaurant wall behind. "This prepares you before you are confronted by the real sea," explains Ibrahim.

It's a theme that Ibrahim follows throughout the entire hotel. Within the spacious suites the palette is ocean-inspired: sand-colored terrazzo tiles are the focus in the bathrooms, and fabrics are locally woven in aquamarine tones. Terracotta blocks depicting Balinese life, dancing and music by Teguh Ostenrik are suitably earthy. Each of the 67 suites has a balcony with ocean view; the higher you are, the better. Furniture was designed with the outdoors in mind. "It's a twist on that famous saying about the Chelsea house where the furniture was in the garden and the drawing room was full of flowers," says Ibrahim, slightly tongue in cheek. Elegant and clean-lined, it has more than a touch of deco to it.

Also ocean-inspired are the restaurant and spa. Seafood beach barbecues on wood grills and ocean-fresh bounty in both the Balinese and Western menus may be enjoyed either al-fresco or in the handsome dining room. And for spa sybarites, there's a line of botanical products specially devised for the hotel by aromatherapist Brenda Ramen. An exciting line-up of treatment packages with themes like Ocean and Earth are unique to the Legian. Appropriately, Ocean starts with a salt scrub and seaweed wrap and ends with a wave massage where you are massaged above and below simultaneously — believe me, it's divine.

Jalan Laksmana, Seminyak Beach, Bali 80361, Indonesia.
tel: +62 361 730 622   fax: +62 361 730 623
legian@ghmhotels.com   www.ghmhotels.com

The Club at the Legian Seminyak

Rising to the challenge for ever more personalized service and total guest privacy, the Legian opened a wonderful series of private residences across the road from their main hotel in 2002. Called the Club at the Legian, it comprises ten one-bedroom villas and one three-bedroom villa, all with private pools set in individual walled compounds. To service these, there's a deluxe clubhouse, with 35-meter (115-foot) lap pool, restaurant and bar — and each villa is provided with a butler. In the words of the general manager: "We set out to offer a completely secluded and private space for two where everything you want is to hand." Sensitively done? Yes. Sensuous? Definitely.

No stone was left unturned in designing a space that is totally indulgent, in terms of service, atmosphere and facilities. Given that the Club does not have the wonderful sea views of the Legian, the intention was to create a mood and setting entirely different from other villas in Bali. Utilizing the services of Shinta Siregar of Bali-based Nexus Architects and interior designer Jaya Ibrahim, the visually elegant rooms ooze understated drama. The interiors have a pan-Asian aesthetic, yet the material palette is traditional Balinese. Coconut wood is used for columns, *benkerai* and *alang-alang* for roofs, woven rattan on the underside of roofs and on the cupboards and terrazzo with shell chips for floors. Nonetheless, the overall effect is unashamedly contemporary.

Each villa has a lounge area *(see left)*, bedroom, airy bathroom, outdoor bath, and an attractive take on the *balé* with a sunken dining table overlooking a plunge pool. There's a fashion-forward feeling permeating throughout: this is achieved by both the mod cons to hand (DVD, TV and CD player with concealed speakers, desk with internet connection, espresso machine and more) and a color palette of dark timbers and black terrazzo. Of particular note are the series of streamlined *banji* screens that run along the outer wall of the villas. Made from mahogany. they allow shadow and light to fall in geometric patterns in the interior. As Ibrahim says: "The villa is completely enclosed, and could be rather claustrophobic. The idea is to bring the world to the guest, rather than having the guest get up and look for it."

Most visitors to the Club are there precisely because they don't want the world to intrude. Their *raison d'etre* is to chill (in private) — and everything is organized so as to facilitate this. The color palette of chocolate brown, cream, biscuit and grey, with soft furnishings in natural *tenun* fabric, are soothing and easy on the eye. CDs and DVDs are available on demand. Bathing options are twofold, in the wickedly self-indulgent outdoor terrazzo tub set in a lily pond, or in the Javanese stone-tiled plunge pool where a sculpture of a stylized offering tray filled with goodies for the gods is given center stage. Meals can be ordered at any time of day or night; all you have to do is dial B for Butler.

Thoughts of shopping along nearby Jalan Seminyak or a trip to the hills (there is a private limousine service at the Club) became more and more remote the longer I stayed. Time and again, the circular outer table with cushions beneath the *balé* roof was the magnet: it is the spot that everyone gravitates toward. And once you're there … why move? Taking meals, reading, or simply idling away the hours, listening to the tinkling water in the ornamental pond, made me lazier and lazier.

If you do get it together to emerge, cocoon-like, from your deluxe hideaway, all the facilities at the Legian are open to Club guests — spa, pool and restaurants. Also, reserved for Club guests only is the private clubhouse, a semi-open, breezy structure where Indonesian shells and glass on the tabletops and bar counter play tricks on the eye and a short, but excellent, menu is served. Here the atmosphere is hushed and somnolent: I never once saw anyone in the pool, and only occasionally someone in the bar … and they were usually either checking in or checking out.

For style aficionados, people wanting to get to know each other better (!) and those in search of solitude, the Club offers a zen-like experience in seriously tasteful surrounds. It's high style hedonistic and deliciously indulgent.

Jalan Laksmana, Seminyak Beach, Bali 80361, Indonesia.
tel: +62 361 730 622   fax: +62 361 730 623
legian@ghmhotels.com   www.ghmhotels.com

Begawan Giri Estate Sayan

There ought to be a warning sign at the entrance to Begawan Giri Estate reading: "Begawan causes total bliss-out. Beware." My advice? Take precautions before you leave home: Don't pack books, laptops, telephone numbers, fancy clothes and makeup. Take only yourself, an open mind and a sarong. On arrival, just give yourself up to the place; don't fight it. The trick is total submission.

So how? Indeed, why? These are difficult questions to answer, because the magic of Begawan lies in simply *being*. But if push comes to shove, I'd say it's because it has elevated the concept of service to an art form in an environment that combines wilderness with refinement. Because the 9 hectares (22 acres) of land comprise a "private estate" rather than a "hotel." Because the warmth of the staff comes from an inner radiance rather than from a learnt code of conduct. Because, once you immerse yourself in the place, you're freed from the normal constraints of a normal hotel — and you can simply be.

If this sounds a bit new agey, it isn't. "First and foremost, Begawan Giri is a home," declares founder Bradley Gardner, "albeit an extremely luxurious one. That's why it's called a private estate, not a hotel." And it pushes the boundaries of hospitality. You, as the guest, are its *raison d'etre.*

It's as if all the irritating quibbles you have about hotels have been erased. For a start, if you're flying into Denpasar, a representative meets you before immigration and fast tracks you through customs and out the airport. When you arrive at the estate, a private butler deals with your passport formalities; he or she unpacks, packs, feeds, clothes, even breathes for you if necessary. You soon discover that you don't have to bother with signing after you have a meal or a drink; your order is just discreetly added to your bill. You don't pay extra for any of the generous

quantities of mineral water left at strategic points in your residence. If you want a special request food-wise, nothing is too much trouble. The air-conditioning is virtually silent; in fact there is no sound of generators, buggies or any machinery. If you want a bath, boiling hot water tumbles out of a bamboo tap into a huge six-ton carved-in-situ rock bathtub. If you want a swim, crystal clear spring-fed pools beckon.

Such are the small details. The bigger picture encompasses, and surpasses, them — if it were possible. Begawan Giri's 22 suites housed in five highly individual residences along with some newer villas are scattered on a precipitous swathe of land above the revered Ayung River outside Ubud. Designed by Malaysian-born architect Cheong Yew Kuan, they overlook a mystical panorama of gorge, rice field and tropical vegetation. At the Estate's heart are a trio of streams, a sacred spring and a cluster of rock pools. The benevolent sounds of water, birdsong and breeze in the trees are a constant. Be it in a glimpse of water tumbling over boulders in the gorge, the flit of a flamboyant butterfly's wing or the unfurling frond of a giant tree fern, the environment soothes, calms and restores.

"Conceiving and building the estate was like climbing up a glacier with my finger nails," remarked Bradley. He and his wife bought the site in 1989, but didn't really know what they were going to do with it. It was only after they "sat the land" — all the while meditating, planning and planting over 2,000 hardwood trees — that they began to get an inkling of what was to come. First came work on the outdoor spa;

water was harnessed into natural pools, decking laid and simple outdoor *balés*
built. Then Yew Kuan's extraordinary vision as to where and how buildings could be
situated was incorporated, and as the gardens matured so did the nuts and bolts of
the resort. The years passed, the trees pushed upward, paths were laid, and form
and beauty were conferred on what was already tantamount to a Garden of Eden.

Today, Begawan Giri Estate is part of Como Hotels & Resorts' portfolio. Como's
mission is "to create bespoke retreats where discerning travelers can connect to
the spirit of an unspoilt and precious destination," so Begawan complements its
other resort properties (including Uma Ubud featured on pages 48–53) admirably.
Its acknowledgement of cultural context, a sensitive aesthetic and plans to incorp-
orate a Shambhala spa are now part of the bigger picture.

Even though the resort has the highest in the world guest to staff ratio, the cuisine
is superb, the spa is healing and nurturing, the architecture is to die for — it is the
natural environment that captures the heart. Succumb to its beauty, let it touch you,
reflect, restore and rejuvenate. You won't regret it. Because even though Begawan's
strap line is "a vow to return often," it could be a once in a lifetime experience.

P O Box 54, Ubud 80570, Bali, Indonesia.
tel: +62 361 978 888   fax: +62 361 978 889
reservations@begawan.com   www.begawan.com

Four Seasons Resort & Spa Sayan

Wallpaper* magazine described this groundbreaking resort outside Ubud as "the hot hotel for the close of the century" — and there is no doubt that it is architecturally unique. Daring, both in terms of its suitability to site and its futuristic design, it is a love it or hate it sort of place. One thing you can't do, however, is ignore it.

Designed in the late 1990s by the studio of Malaysian-born British architect, John Heah, the resort is like an inverse high-rise. You enter at the top via a 55-meter (180-foot) elevated teak-and-steel walkway from the Sayan ridge, and proceed down through five floors of a monumental elliptical structure to the valley floor. Each level affords breathtaking views across valley, gorge, river and rice field, in an ever-descending, heady spiral. Once grounded, 28 villas scattered amongst imaginative gardens, continue the downward trend. Access to these is via a *balé* on the roof, from where a circular staircase leads down to the rooms; emerging one floor down onto a patio, it is down some stairs again to the Ayung River's edge.

Extremely controversial during construction (after all is a five-story flying saucer-shaped structure really appropriate in a pristine and sacred river valley?), the hotel has weathered over time. Natural ivory-toned cladding has acquired an attractive darker patina, the gardens and paddy fields have grown in, and the extremely strong architectural presence of the main building is no longer so starkly visible from the surrounding vegetation. A plethora of water features — a massive lotus and lily pond on the entrance roof, ponds on the villa roofs, a number of plunge pools, inclined walls oozing moss and water lining the corridors, and a freeform, double-level riverside swimming pool — further help the buildings merge into the landscape.

The architect clearly liked to juxtapose natural and man-made materials. The stunning central atrium building which houses the lobby, bar, restaurant, spa and fitness center, and has suites radiating from it, is as dramatic for its views as it is for its architecture. Sitting in the Jati Bar where an extensive wine cellar helps to lubricate and relax guests, looking out between stone columns over a panoramic jungle vista is about as good as it gets. Similarly on ground level the villas are interspersed amongst paddy fields and vegetable plots, rather than in manicured tropical gardens.

There are a number of accommodation options, both in the main building off mossy walkways and in villas. A batch of 14 stand-alone villas above the entrance-way is a newer addition. Designed by Cheong Yew Kuan, they are more mini-houses than villas, and would do well for larger groups or families. The valley villas, on the other hand, have easy access to the river and adjacent freeform swimming pool, with a large outside terrace, private plunge pool, and sumptuous bedroom and bathroom. I didn't see many people making use of the lily pond and *balé* on the roof though. Of the 18 suites in the main block, the nicest are the two-level suites: these are slightly smaller than the other rooms, but because they are split level, they have a bit more character. Double-height windows are an added bonus.

As is the norm in all Four Seasons properties, standards of service are very high. Four Seasons prides itself on its highly personalized, anticipatory service; a

recent annual report notes: "Simply put, we treat others — partners, customers, co-workers, everyone — as we would wish them to treat us." This is evident at the Sayan property: members of staff appear to genuinely enjoy working in such an unusual and gorgeous location, and your wish really is their command.

The big bonus, though, is simply *being* in the heart of Bali: its culture, landscape, religion and mystery is as central to the Four Seasons experience here as is the fast-flowing Ayung River. The Balinese have been dipping into this river to purify, wash and nourish for centuries, and the tradition continues today. Adjacent the property, a vertiginous stairway leads down from the ridge above to the valley floor, and local people continue to use this as if there were no tourists, no five-star hotel, no modern architectural edifice in sight. Offerings are laid at the water's edge and in the five temple shrines as they have been for eons. Sarong-clad beauties bathe, and small children caper in the shallows. Life's natural cycle continues — a joyous celebration of nature and the gods — and the hotel simply exists within it.

Sayan, Ubud, Gianyar, Bali 84571, Indonesia.
tel: +62 361 977 577   fax: +62 361 977 588
www.fourseasons.com

Uma Ubud Campuhan

The word "*uma*" translates as "living house" in Bahasa, the Indonesian national language. Significantly it also means "light" in Sanskrit and is an alternative name of the Hindu goddess Parvati. The word is associated with Buddhist philosophy too. With such credentials, it is an apt name for the new line of inland retreat-style hotels launched by Christina Ong's Como group.

Presently, there are two Uma hotels — this one in Bali and a second one in Bhutan. It is no coincidence that they are located in culturally rich spiritual heart-lands, as their intention is to "immerse guests in the textural richness of the resort's carefully chosen region — from culture to religion and landscape — offering the dual experience of escape and adventure." This experience is furthered at both resorts by expansive Shambhala spas where yoga and other programs are offered, an inspiring range of excursions and an uplifting natural environment.

The atmosphere at Uma Ubud is in keeping with this aim. Quiet and secluded, it is situated outside the town on a steep site overlooking the divine Campuhan valley. A celestial vista of rice paddy, coconut palm and river gorge is to be had from most parts of the resort; within, tropical planting, a restrained building ethic and comfortable, but stylish, interiors predominate. This is Bali at its best. The traffic-clogged streets and conspicuous consumerism of the south is far away; art flourishes, as does a thriving culture complete with ritual, dance performances, theater and temple attendance.

Built along the lines of a traditional Balinese village in the hills, Uma Ubud aims to be both ecologically sound and culturally appropriate to setting. Buildings are simple: using wood, *alang-alang* and local stone, the landscape is generously given center stage. Interiors, likewise, are pared-down. Japanese designer Koichiro

Ikebuchi of the Ikebuchi Atelier blends a Zen simplicity with natural materials, all the while harnessing light and air flows in the rooms. Public buildings are similarly tranquil, yet modish. This is a more ascetic design than that found at other Como hotels and resorts, but it is entirely in keeping with the mind/body/spirit ethos of the Uma brand.

The property comprises 29 rooms and suites, three with individual infinity-edge plunge pools. All have garden terraces or private courtyards and facilities include TVs, DVD players, safe, yoga mat and minibar. Some villas have open-air bathrooms that are decadent in their details with custom-crafted tubs, stools covered in *poleng* (black-and-white check) cloth and floaty mosquito envelope. This isn't as daft as it sounds: the baths are open to the elements, and a protective cover isn't such a bad idea. The fact that they look totally gorgeous is an added bonus.

The hotel prides itself on its local knowledge and local staff. Tailor-made excursions are designed to help visitors appreciate the truly magical milieu they've found themselves in. Bespoke cultural tours include visits to local museums, artists' studios and temples, while courses on a range of activities, including Indonesian batik, puppet making, mask painting and Balinese cookery, can be organized. Special week-long yoga retreats and physical training challenge weeks are offered, as are a range of more activity-oriented excursions: guided walks, mountain biking, volcano runs and white-water rafting. Each day guests are briefed of any special local events taking place.

This resort is clearly aimed at stressed urbanites desirous of something more than a sun, sea and sand break. If you want to learn a little (nothing too educational though, you understand!), love a little and chill more than a little — this could be just the Indonesian idyll you've been searching for. It isn't really a kids' place, it has to be said, so honeymooners and couples should take note. Whether you are practising yoga in an out-jutting voluminous pavilion or relaxing in the lakeside restaurant, you'll be drinking in vertiginous views over the valley and luxuriating in the power of near-silent stillness. It is a exhilarating combination.

The message at Uma Ubud is about discovery. Forget the coast, forget the traffic, put a block on the mayhem outside the resort walls: spend time with yourself or a loved one, and you may find a bit more. About the island, about the culture — or even about yourself.

Jalan Raya Sanggingan, Banjar Lungsiakan, Kedewatan,
Ubud, Gianyar 80571, Bali, Indonesia.
tel: +62 361 972 448
info.ubud@uma.como.bz   www.uma.como.bz

Alila Jakarta

When Alila Jakarta opened in 2001, it was a first for the capital. Most Indonesians equate luxury with opulence and international brands, so the understated style of the hotel came as a surprise. Where were the artworks, the huge floral arrangements, the fuss, the clutter? Why didn't the GM wear a suit and tie? Why was the Buzz restaurant called a café? Where was the banqueting hall? It took them a while to get used to the new concept of geometry, space and simplicity — but over time, Jakartans began to see its merits, and pragmatically took to its low-key vibe.

In fact, the hotel was born of pragmatism, with owner Franky Tjahyadikarta openly admitting that the original plan was for something far more conventional. But with the economic downturn demanding cost cutting, he decided to set his vision inward. "I slashed the budget, changed the design, and worked with the architect and his team to come up with something far less glitzy, but much more modern," he says. "Thus the concept of Alila came about."

Alila is a Sanskrit word for "surprise," and the hotel is surprising on many levels. Even though its style (or lack of it) was born of necessity, it has bred well — and business is booming. "It took a while to educate people as to what we were about," says the general manager, but hey, when you have a car showroom on the ground floor, what can you expect?

Admittedly this is one of the hotel's quirkier aspects. But from the second floor up, Alila is all about forward-looking hoteliering. Behind an imposing grey concrete exterior of two 27-story towers lies a striking modernity. Conceptualized by architect Budiman Hendropurnomo of local firm Denton Corker Marshall, first impressions reveal strong geometric forms and an efficient aesthetic. Black granite floors, huge mirrors, clean-lined seating and a giant contemporary artwork of colored wood

strips by Pieter Dietmar characterize the lobby lounge. Softened only by a wave-like ceiling pattern and intermittent splashes of color, the lounge overlooks a Japanese-inspired court with frangipani trees and grey pebbled hardscape. This serves to bring natural light into the double-height space.

Because of the lack of adornment, you tend to notice the little things — the sinuous curves of an armchair, a pattern of light and shade falling on a wall or the design magazines provided in the upper Space lounge. Other thoughtful touches include rooms with high-speed internet access (this is free in the suites), wireless access in the public spaces, a very large gym, spacious Mandara spa, and casual yet trendy staff uniforms. Casual yet trendy staff too. The overall feeling is relaxed, young, pared down — without distractions. An added boon for single women travelers is a special Executive Ladies Floor with extra security, female butlers on call 24 hours a day, access with a separate key card, and special ladies' amenities.

Guest rooms, which range in size from 37 to 84 sq meters (400 to 900 sq feet), are unembellished — but unblemished. Warm *merbau* wood floors, saffron-hued cushions and covers, custom-designed furniture and sizeable bathrooms with all amenities are practical — yet comfortable. An over long, slim desk is perfect for the busy exec, while the design conscious will appreciate the suede and synthetic leather sofa, ottoman and chairs. Magnificent floor-to-ceiling glass windows and doors to a small balcony give uninterrupted views over the city center — especially if you are on one of the higher floors. Earplugs may be in order though, as there is a mosque with muezzin just across the street.

Food at Alila Jakarta is unpretentious too. Buzz Wine & Dine has black tables of anodized copper, *nyatoh* timber chairs and an open-plan, snappy kitchen serving Japanese, Mediterranean and Asian cuisine. If you prefer to eat in the Space lounge, that's fine too. In fact, anything goes. "We just want people to feel relaxed," says the suitably suave general manager, "for the most part, our clientele is pretty low key; they like things uncomplicated — simplicity is an important part of the Alila ethos."

Behind this apparent simplicity, however, lies a slick operation. In addition to the two existing properties in Bali (Alila Manggis and Alila Ubud) and this Jakarta one, there are new villas in Thailand, and plans for other properties in Southeast Asia. Commitment to cheerful, relaxed service is key, as is the idea of space. Indeed, at Alila Jakarta, even when the hotel is full, it never seems crowded. That is a rare achievement in a 164-room hotel in a city center.

Jalan Pecenongan Kav 7–17, Jakarta 10120, Indonesia.
tel: +62 21 231 6008   fax: +62 21 231 6007
jakarta@alilahotels.com   www.alilahotels.com

The Dharmawangsa Jakarta

The arm of the Dharmawangsa's exclusivity extends even into Jakarta airport where a representative of the hotel meets guests prior to customs and immigration. He welcomes you, takes your passport, whisks you past queues of people, gets your passport stamped, organizes your luggage — and within moments you're in the latest BMW or a classic Bentley heading into town. The airport boulevard, lined on either side by fish farms, half-completed buildings, and the sight of hundreds of kites flying in the sky, is a blur. You are relaxing in the back, playing with the gizmos (if you're a guy), checking out the magazines (if you're a girl) and luxuriating in the fact that everyone else on your plane is still waiting in line at immigration.

"A stay at the Dharmawangsa starts with the transfer," explains the general manager, "so we like to pick guests up wherever they are. It is part of the overall Dharmawangsa experience."

If you think this is sound, sensible, pampering and kind — wait until you reach the hotel itself. Situated in the prestigious Kebayoran Baru residential district south of the city center, the hotel is set just back from a quiet shady street in an ample garden setting. An open columned verandah leads into a marble-cool front lobby, where superlative smiles, friendly faces and a chorus of *selamats* greet you. Then it is just a quick walk to your room or suite for in-room check-in. The mesmeric scent of jasmine hangs in the air as large ceramic pots full of the blooms are artfully arranged on long fan-shaped sticks.

As befits both location and concept, the hotel has a distinctly residential feel. Designed to showcase the many facets of both modern and ancient Indonesia, the Dharmawangsa consists of a series of linked spaces with a central atrium and four lounges at its center. Dharmawangsa was an 11th century Hindu king from East Java who laid the foundations of the great Majapahit Empire — so it is fitting that the hotel's interior design pays tribute to the extraordinary artistic achievements of the era.

The heart and soul of the hotel consists of the central Majapahit Hall. Here, two musicians and a stall serving Javan sweetmeats and teas flank an obelisk with 14th century temple decoration. Off this hall radiate four lounges, sumptuously decorated by interior design maestro Jaya Ibrahim. The tea lounge is all colonial rattan, swaying palm fronds, dappled light and shade from Venetian blinds, linen napkins and silver service. The adjacent library with floor-to-ceiling book shelves and custom-carved cabinetry is a clubby mix of dark green silk and amber upholstery, while the caviar lounge showcases a priceless collection of antique jewelry from Sumatra set in 25 glass cases on a silk covered wall *(see left)*. Adjacent this is the bar, where chocolate martinis and cigars from the well-stocked humidor are the order of the evening.

For me, this series of rooms represents everything that is truly perfect about the Dharmawangsa. From air-conditioning concealers crafted in a metal grid fashioned after the *cemukiran* motif (a pattern on a Javanese ceremonial garment) to heavy metal lights in the shape of the sun, the symbol of the Majapahit Empire, every detail is meticulously thought through. Each piece of custom-crafted furniture and artwork has a cultural reference — be it the three-legged Pesisiran (coastal) armchair, carved wooden screens or terracotta tablets copied from the Penataran temple of East Java. Furthermore, exquisite antiques collected from all over the archipelago — from betel nut sets to water carriers, plates and jars — bear the mark of sophisticated workmanship.

The 100 rooms and suites are no less impressive: Featuring fabrics, artifacts, prints and paintings, as well as a specific color scheme, they represent five areas of the Indonesian archipelago — Nusa Tenggara, Java, Bali, Pesisiran and Sumatra. Each is noteworthy for the sumptuousness of its furniture and furnishings, huge balconies, exceptional amenities, the services of a 24-hour butler, cavernous bathrooms with Lady Primrose toiletries, and magnificent complimentary chocolate sculpture and bottle of champagne. If you want to feel truly pampered and cosseted, the two penthouse suites with wrap-around balconies, private Jacuzzis and a series of interlinked rooms are difficult to beat. The townhouse suites on the ground floor are a personal favorite: duplex-like, with bedroom above and lounge below, they have immediate access to the leafy garden.

But really, it doesn't matter which room you take: in keeping with the Rosewood hotel philosophy of "offering exceptional service, a luxury product and incredible attention to detail," Dharmawangsa delivers. And in the same way that Rosewood has a collection of hotels rather than a chain, the Dharmawangsa feels like a residence, rather than a hotel. I will definitely be back.

Jalan Brawijawa Raya no 26, Jakarta 12160, Indonesia.
tel: +62 21 725 8181   fax: +21 725 8383
www.rosewoodhotels.com

Amanjiwo near Borobudur

It's clear as soon as you arrive at Amanjiwo that your experience will be a cultural
one. Every aspect and activity at the resort celebrates either the nearby Buddhist
monument of Borobudur or the physical and cultural heritage of Java. The connection to both land and people is more than an architectural one — indeed the hotel
excels in creating innovate ways in which to showcase Java in its many forms. And
by doing so, it lures you into its mystical, secretive landscape and people — so
much so that you won't want to leave.

There is an overwhelming sense of serenity about Amanjiwo: the gentle staff
who never fail to address you by name with the Javanese *ibu* or *bapak* nomen-
clature, the secluded location sheltered by the Menorah hills and the sounds of the
gamelan permeate into your unconscious. Before you know it, you have slowed
down, your voice has become softer, you start to stroll rather than stride. It isn't
for nothing, you come to realize, that Amanjiwo translates as "peaceful soul."

Designed by Ed Tuttle in a setting that offers views of four volcanoes as well as
Borobudur itself, Amanjiwo's architecture takes its cue from the motifs of the nearby
Buddhist monument. At its heart lies a spherical rotunda with bell-shaped roof; at
a point half way down the steep drive Borobudur itself is framed through the building's center. The rest of the resort fans out from this central axis: 36 suites over two
deep crescents, 14 swimming pools, private gardens, the hotel's 40-meter (130-foot)
main pool and colonnaded pool club, as well as the two-bedroom Dalem Jiwo suite.
All is crafted from local limestone hewn from the Menorah hills: soft, gleaming, therapeutic even, its pale tones absorb the clean air and seem to reflect it out again.

Walled suites are simple, yet sumptuous. Sliding screens of *sunkai* wood with
perforated triangle shapes echoing the patterns of Borobudur's 72 smaller stupas

separate the dressing room and outdoor bathroom from the bedroom. Here a pillared central bed on a terrazzo platform is the main feature. Lying on ours, looking over plunge pool and private pavilion or *kubuk* and across tobacco fields to Borobudur, was exhilarating and entirely appropriate. Rooms don't have TVs, but are equipped with music systems, the usual amenities, (telephone) internet access, coconut wood and rattan furniture, traditional reverse paintings on glass and daybeds outside for lounging. Of particular note is the outside terrazzo tub. Take a tip: go for an evening soak illuminated by moon and candlelight and listen to the sounds of the Javan night.

The emphasis at Amanjiwo is on the creative excursions organized by the staff. Personalized attention ensures that you feel like an intrepid explorer or a cultural tourist — never a mass tourist. Tailor-made to suit individual requirements, each trip surprises with its minute attention to every detail. Most guests opt to view Borobudur at sunrise and many come back by elephant. Both come highly recommended, but I suggest you don't miss out on the secluded breakfast on a hillock overlooking the monument. What could beat a picnic with steaming hot Javan coffee, fresh fruit, bacon and ciabatta sandwiches, and a private viewing of the eighth wonder of the Oriental world framed by ancient pine trees? You may even be inspired to use the watercolors and sketchpad so thoughtfully provided.

Other more energetic excursions offer full-moon volcano climbing, treks in the hills as well as visits to the Yogyakarta *kraton* and bespoke shopping trips. Sipping Amanjiwo's signature sour sop martini atop the Menorah hills or on a grassy plateau in the rice fields at sunset is deliciously indulgent. Other daily activities that anchor the hotel experience with a sense of place (an integral part of the Aman experience) are the daily visit of a village *ibu*, who brings her home-made herbal tonics and teas with her, children's dances in the main rotunda at tea-time, the services of a Javanese elder educated in the traditional *pijat* therapeutic massage, and nightly *gamelan* music. Honeymooners, and special guests, may experience the lavish *selematan* in the Dalem Jiwo suite: here a 10-person *gamelan* orchestra and trance-dancers perform, while you eat a traditional banquet beneath the central Javan star-studded sky. It's a memorable evening.

Whatever your preference — a game of tennis, a trek, a lounge, or a quiet evening in your suite — you can be sure of one thing. It takes place against a backdrop of humility, warmth and openness. Amanjiwo's staff is, quite simply, amongst the best anywhere — and a fitting tribute to both Aman Resorts and Java itself.

Borobudur, Central Java, Indonesia.
tel: +62 293 788 333   fax: +62 293 788 355
amanjiwo@amanresorts.com   www.amanresorts.com

Rumah Sleman Yogyakarta

A sedate-paced *andong* (horse-and-buggy) ride through the country villages around Yogyakarta is the perfect excursion. An air-con jeep is too modern, bicycles too hot, and if you walk, you don't see enough. Whereas the *andong* … it's open-air, it's picturesque, it sort of fits in with the surroundings. Which are a peek at life lived slowly, lived naturally, lived a little in the past. An old man pulls on a cheroot, children run out waving as you clip-clop past, drying rice grains are laid out on mats, and rice fields are at the point of no return. Each stalk is ready for threshing; it leans against its neighbor with head hanging, pleading for the picking. All is green, everything fresh.

Half an hour later, you can stop at the market to buy ingredients for a traditional Javanese cooking lesson back at the ranch — or you can head home to relax. For Rumah Sleman is a home (*rumah* means "house" in Javanese, Sleman is the area in which it is situated). With only four suites, a wonderful wrap-around verandah, country views, an extraordinary reception area in the form of a royal *pendopo*, personalized service, heritage furniture, and a tranquil, otherworldly atmosphere, this is unlike any other home you'll have stayed in. It has one foot in the present, one in the past.

Situated on the outskirts of Yogyakarta, 15 minutes from the airport, 15 minutes from the *kraton* (royal court) and 35 minutes from the Buddhist monument of Borobudur, Rumah Sleman is little advertised and little known. If you manage to book a suite here, keep your eyes closed as the car pulls through the gate for the first time. When you open them, prepare to be amazed. In front of you is a voluminous wooden structure known as a *pendopo*: built in 1814 for the royal family of Kasunanan in Solo (Surakarta) and transported to the present site in 1998, it is intricately carved beneath a soaring *joglo* roof. A red carpet strewn with jasmine leads into the traditional reception room known as a *ndalem*: here a pair of *loro blonyoh* figures (painted statues in bridal attire) sits beneath a stunning crystal chandelier before a gorgeous carved screen (*gebyok*). There is more red carpet, more jasmine petals and the fragrance of tuberose. You are given a wonderful ginger tea — and smiles, handshakes and cool towels ensure the welcome is fit for a king.

This is apt, as the *pendopo* and house behind it is owned by the widow of the grandson of the tenth sultan of Surakarta, Paku Buwono — and a collection of his furniture, bearing the royal insignia, is found inside. The house itself is a newly built villa in neo-colonial Dutch style where modern amenities, such as near silent air-con and luxuriously appointed marble bathrooms, mingle with priceless antiques. Imaginatively formulated by two of Jakarta's leading interior designers, you can choose to stay in a Western-style suite or a Javanese-style one. Both are totally gorgeous — the only advice I can offer is to go by instinct.

The sister-in-law of owner Ibu Ana Bambang Surjo Sunindar manages the property. "Our idea here," explains Ibu Meiske Mathovani, "is to make guests feel comfortable and welcome. We find out what food they like, what they prefer to drink, what they enjoy doing, then we organize it for them." Rumah Sleman's usual activities include Javanese cooking lessons, traditional spa treatments and excursions to surrounding tourist sites, but if you are so inclined, staff can organize an authentic Javanese wedding ceremony. Priests, musicians, traditional attire, banquets — no problem! "If you are already married, but want a second ceremony, that is possible too," says Ibu Meiske with a smile.

If it's just a straightforward holiday you require, there is no better place for it. You have the services of a 24-hour butler, private chef and the most wonderful surroundings on hand. There's a formal dining room with crystal lights, huge table and grand piano; comfortable verandah with pool table and tinkling fountain; a gazebo in the garden for breakfast; and rice field and jungle views. Idiosyncratic touches include a Trussardi bicycle with leather saddle, framed letters from previous sultans and dignitaries such as Stamford Raffles, family portraits, mirrors bearing the royal crown insignia, an antique Javanese sitar and an amazing collection of Murano glassware. A swimming pool is a possibility in the future.

My favorite room was the Jaya Ibrahim-designed deep blue-and-rust double bedroom with private verandah *(see overleaf)*. Here Chinese antique ceramics are displayed on the walls and occasional tables, and an antique silver tea set sits at the foot of the bed on a silver platter. Double doors with carved lintels lead to a verandah where deep, low, colonial leather-and-cane armchairs afford views of singing birds and garden. Alternatively, you can opt for the Ted Sulisto-designed quarters where high, dark wood beds with cushions stitched with Ibu Ana's initials and *toile de Jouy* bedspreads offer opulence and comfort *(this page)*. It's not an easy choice.

Jalan Purboyo No 111, Warak Kidul, Sumberadi, Sleman, Yogyakarta, Indonesia.
tel: +62 274 866 611/22   fax: +62 274 866 633
rumahsleman@hotmail.com   www.rumahsleman.com

Losari Magelang

If Java is synonymous with coffee, then Losari is the place to experience it. Part plantation, part resort, part mist, part mountain, Losari Coffee Plantation & Spa perches on a breezy 22 hectares (55 acres) of land within its own Ring of Fire. No less than eight volcanoes encircle it, including the still active Merapi — and views of four of them are best had from the resort's suites. Sipping a cup of unfiltered coffee *tubruk* on your balcony with volcanic views is both awesome and relaxing: all you need to consider is what you want to do next: a stroll, tennis, or a spot of lunch?

The alternative is to simply kick back and do nothing. Losari is very good for that. The serenity of central Java's luxuriant landscape is conducive to meditative moments. Contemplating life, its meaning and the universe are appropriate to setting and situation. After all, the Javanese believe that their island is where heaven and earth are closest, with the volcanoes acting as celestial go-betweens. And not far from Losari million-year-old fossils of Java man or *Homo erectus* were excavated at Sangiran village. It would not be inaccurate to say that man was born nearby.

If that doesn't blow your mind, everything else about Losari will. The brainchild (or perhaps love child?) of Italian designer Gabriella Teggia, Losari is brimming with beauty. At its center lies an 1820s Dutch villa on a hillock; ample verandahs with colonial rattan-and-wood rocking chairs afford vistas over the resort's traditional Javanese public buildings and villas, to rice paddy, forest and volcanoes beyond. Aptly enough, this original plantation *landhuis*, with its overhanging eaves, imposing pillars, antique furniture, library and music room, is the focal point of the resort.

Gabriella obtained the site in 1992 and spent the next few years revitalizing the coffee plantation, renovating the manor house and scouring the country for traditional pavilions and houses earmarked for destruction. She bought them, had them dis-

mantled and transported to Losari and then reconstructed them as close to their original specifications as possible. Take the cluster of *pendopos* or pavilions that constitute bar, restaurant and *gamelan* stage: with symbolic mathematical construction, intricate carving and soaring hipped *joglo*-style roofs in local clay tiles, they're an inspiring showcase of Javan craftsmanship.

No less impressive are the 26 suites housed in individual villas scattered around the 900-meter (2,950-foot) high plantation. Situated so as to make the most of volcano views, each has an extremely spacious interior decked out with a hybrid mix of furniture including four-poster bed and lounging daybed, soft cottons and individual art pieces. Hand-painted shutters, old armoires to conceal TV and DVD players, interior carving, as well as bathrooms with one-of-a-kind tubs crafted from lava stone, blue mosaic tiles, or beaten copper, are highly individualistic. Of particular note is the Bela Vista suite housed in an old prince's residence transported from the *kraton* (court) of Solo. This comes with its own private pool with Italianate gargoyles.

Guests in other suites need not fret, as there is a huge infinity-edge pool, a spa with two Turkish *hamams*, an excellent choice of scrubs, potions and lotions, and both *pijat* and long-stroke massage. For the more energetic, Losari can organize dawn trips to Borobudur and other temples, sightseeing tours of Semarang, Yogya and Surakarta (Solo), as well as volcano climbing, trekking and shopping trips. You can even experience a short ride on a 1902 steam train through the rice fields.

Losari works closely with the surrounding villagers, artisans and farmers — and 60 percent of the staff comes from the nearby village. It operates a foundation to improve infrastructure, schools and other projects in the area, and often hosts cultural evenings of local music and dance. A village lady prepares *jamu* (Javan herbal medicine) in the traditional manner every morning and walks around the plantation with her teas and tonics in a basket on her back: believed to keep people young, healthy and virile, unlike many *jamus* it doesn't taste too bad either. Also, during the coffee harvest, guests are invited to join in if they wish.

There is also an eco emphasis in the operations. Losari (which means "essence of trees") has over 2,200 trees on site, nearly 50 different varieties of bamboo, a koi pond and other water features, as well as fields of organic fruit and vegetables. Sensible waste practice and recycling is not neglected and fresh water from the plantation spring is used whenever possible. Coffee is grown without the use of pesticides or chemicals. This sustainable emphasis, along with the showcasing of Java's heritage and the lush local scenery, makes Losari unique. Book early.

PO Box 108, Magelang 56100, Central Java, Indonesia.
tel: +62 298 596 333   fax: +62 298 592 696
info@losaricoffeeplantation.com   www.losaricoffeeplantation.com

Cheong Fatt Tze Mansion   Penang

It's always a good sign when a prompt, friendly reply comes back from an email requesting a room reservation. It's even better when the person suggests what type of room would be best, says a credit card number isn't necessary to secure the room, and writes: "How will you be coming up? Do let me know what your plans are … any questions you have, please throw them this way." How refreshing, I thought. Informal, accommodating, welcoming … just like the hotel itself, as it turned out.

For a two-day trip to Penang to check out conservation and restoration projects in the old trading post of Georgetown, I'd chosen to stay at Cheong Fatt Tze Mansion. Known to locals as The Blue House on Leith Street, it is a dazzling, indigo-blue late 19th century heritage home that has been meticulously restored and found new life as a small boutique hotel. With 38 rooms, four courtyards and seven staircases, it offers guest accommodation in 16 rooms, all with en suite bathrooms. A delicious full breakfast is served adjacent the open-to-the-sky central courtyard beneath cooling fans, but no other meals are offered. Nonetheless, Cheong Fatt Tze offers a type of old-fashioned, personalized hospitality that is increasingly rare nowadays.

Manager Rami Nuek and her staff are friendly and full of information. Nothing seems too much trouble, and Nuek will always take time out to chat. I requested the services of a foot reflexologist one evening, and she asked "When?"; I replied "Now?" and she didn't bat an eyelid! She promised to see what she could do, then phoned the room two minutes later to tell me that the appointment was arranged for half an hour's time. Similarly, travel arrangements, recommendations for local and international restaurants and tourist information were given generously.

No doubt it's such service that led US-based, Australian writer Peter Carey to declare: "This is the best hotel in the whole world!" But he was surely influenced by

the building as well: It is, quite simply, in a league of its own. One of only a handful of such mansions still in existence, the house was built over a period of 20 years commencing in the 1880s, by a Chinese tycoon and Manchu official named Cheong Fatt Tze. Incorporating elements of the Chinese courtyard house with its rigid *feng shui* principles with Eastern and Western decorative embellishments, it combines airy, open, almost casual, spaces with impressive, formal reception rooms.

When the present owners acquired the house, it was in a shocking state of deterioration. Co-owner Lawrence Loh, who was educated at nearby St Xavier's and passed it every day on his way back from school, said he felt "the house literally calling out to me." Decades of squatters, the harsh tropical climate and years of neglect had reduced the once-glorious mansion to "a filthy, derelict shell." Restoration took place over a period of six years, and was done in as authentic a manner as was conceivably possible. Utilizing traditional tools, local artisans and craftsmen from China repaired the timberworks and re-crafted the external *chien nien* or cut-and-paste porcelain shard artworks; the original ironwork from the McFarlane foundry in Glasgow was cleaned and repaired whilst missing ironwork was cast locally; a stained-glass specialist spent over three years restoring, replacing and re-crafting the exquisite collection of Art Nouveau stained glass that filled the Gothic windows. Painstaking cleaning of tiles and gold leaf decoration, and a faithful restoration of *trompe l'oeil* beams and paint and plaster finishes completed the gargantuan task.

The result is a building emotionally and physically in keeping with the spirit in which it was built. Cheong Fatt Tze had reputedly declared that he wanted his house to be filled with life and people, so it was decided that the mansion should re-open — not as a sterile museum to the past, but as a living, breathing small-scale hotel. However, twice-daily tours are conducted for both hotel guests and non-residents, and these are fascinating explorations of both past lives and the house's present incarnation. They are non-intrusive, and focus mainly on the public spaces, as well as rooms that have been specifically stocked with Cheong's family memorabilia: old photos, clothes, furniture and his will.

Not surprisingly, the US$2 million restoration project has been the recipient of both the Malaysian National Architectural Award for Conservation and UNESCO's first Asia-Pacific Heritage Conservation Award bestowed in 2001. Both were well deserved — and the Blue House is a delightful place to stay to boot.

14 Leith Street, 10200 Penang, Malaysia.
tel/fax: +60 4 262 5289
cftm@tm.net.my   www.cheongfatttzemansion.com

Eastern & Oriental Hotel Penang

Billed in its heyday as the "premier hotel east of Suez," Penang's Eastern & Oriental hotel oozes history, opulence and glamor. Behind a profusion of domes, minarets, arches, pillars, columns and cornices, is a substantial product. With 101 suites, an extremely long seafront overlooking the Straits of Penang, 24-hour butler service, a variety of eating and drinking venues, as well as a colonial-style atmosphere, the E & O straddles past and present with panache. For the architectural history buff, it rocks; and for those who want modern-day amenities, they won't be disappointed either.

This hasn't always been the case, as the hotel has had a chequered history. Starting life as a 30-bedroom lodging house in the 1880s, it was one of the astute Armenian Sarkies brothers' ventures. Even though it was modest to begin with (it only expanded to 80 rooms in about 1903), the hostelry had a glorious sea view. Presiding over the harbor where a myriad of vessels oiled the wheels of colonial commerce, it gradually gained in popularity and amenities. By 1923, money had been spent on improvements, and the E & O came into its own.

The next few years saw the hotel's glory years. Nightly dances, masked balls and legendary parties with celebrated guests epitomized the zenith of the British Empire. The ballroom was the venue for the colonials' main social events, the annual St George's Day Ball for the English and the St Andrew's Day Ball for the Scots, not to mention the Christmas and New Year parties. The hotel's glittering halls were filled to the rafters with revelers. Naturally nobody was vulgar enough to pay cash; rather they signed "chits" on credit — and some unfortunately amassed huge debts. It was at this time that one clever wag nicknamed the E & O "the Eat and Owe!"

However, its tenure at the center of Penang's glittering social life was short lived. Proprietor Arshak Sarkies over-stretched both himself and his budgets, and the balls, banquets and boozing came to a sorry end in 1931 when the business went bankrupt. After occupation by the Japanese during World War 11, the hotel's fortunes waxed and waned but it never managed to re-capture the heady élan of the 1920s.

Until 2001, that is. Because that was the year this grand old lady reopened her doors after a five-year restoration job that cost US$20 million. From the minute you enter the forecourt with its Victorian wrought iron pillars, and swish through the revolving doors attended by a doorman in colonial attire (think khaki shorts and shirt with pith helmet, long socks and gloves), you know you're entering another world. All the elegance and atmosphere of the E & O's past is preserved in the setting, but the bricks and mortar have been thoroughly updated and modernized. This is evident in the facilities too: a dinner à deux, for example, in the formal dining room where exquisite French cuisine is served, is a languorous affair. When I visited, the night was made all the more memorable with fine wine, excellent service and the best langoustine I'd had in eons.

The E & O was always famous for its steel-domed reception area and this has been retained, along with Carrera marble floors and cupola above, as the hotel's central hub. On one side is a grand staircase, while on the other a curved reception desk in *nyatoh* and *merbau* timbers: here you are received before entering the original Otis cage lift, the first to be installed in Malaya, to be whisked up to your suite. This, naturally, is supremely comfortable, and either affords a view over the Straits of Penang or across the tiled roofs of Georgetown's many preserved buildings. If it's a larger one, you'll have your own private garden terrace, but highly recommended are the Writer's Suites: Named after former guests Rudyard Kipling, Noel Coward, Somerset Maugham and Herman Hesse, these have their own dining room and lounge with bar as well.

The interiors are more British country house than Eastern or Oriental — and this is how it should be. Antique and reproduction Victorian furniture in the form of huge armoires, four-poster beds and ornate desks hark back to a former era, while potted palms, original ceiling fans and choice accents anchor the rooms with a sense of place. Bathrooms with black-and-white tiles, brass taps, English toiletries and monogrammed towels are colonial chic. It isn't difficult to dream yourself back in time: after all, a planter or a visiting dignitary from abroad may have occupied your suite in the past. Pre-dinner drinks (think gin slings, tumblers of whisky and

the like) would have been imbibed, a Charleston practiced, and maybe even a private soirée held within its confines. Many a guest, fresh off the boat from Europe, allowed the ambience of the E & O to go to their head.

Certainly guests would have availed themselves of a promenade along the seafront, and this is as popular a pastime today as it was in earlier eras. During the renovation, the gardens were given a thorough makeover: new ixora and jasmine shrubs were planted, the swimming pool was enlarged, and the embankment seawall was heightened. Still, many of the old features remain: ancient cannon bought by the Sarkies still point out to sea, a Java olive tree planted before 1885 continues to cast shade and the palm-fringed views are as evocative as ever. When strolling through these peaceful surrounds, it is easy to see why the E & O was once known as the "Pearl of the Orient."

Today, its pristine white-painted façade is a landmark sight in the UNESCO World Heritage site of Georgetown. Proudly standing before blue sea and horizon, it once again welcomes guests from across the seas. Long may it continue.

10 Farquhar Street, 10200 Penang, Malaysia.
tel: +60 4 222 2000   fax: +60 4 261 6333
hotel-info@e-o-hotel.com   www.e-o-hotel.com

Four Seasons Resort & Spa Langkawi

With a beachfront that exceeds — by miles (literally) — any other hotel in Asia, this resort is a haven for sea, sun and sand sybarites. It is also great for spa go-ers. There is superb beach service (think comfy loungers, cool scented towels, ice-cold drinks), stunning views out to an emerald ocean dotted with rocky islet, a plethora of water sports and fabulous sunsets overlooking the Andaman Sea. This is Asia's (not Malaysia's) premier property for the sun-seeker.

But we aren't talking Nice or Cannes here, you understand. If you are after nightlife and the high life, heard further north to the sin spots of Pattaya or Phuket. There, the bars are open all night. Langkawi's gorgeous strip of white sand meets glittering sea at Tanjung Rhu is more in the style of a rustic Riviera. Within the resort are shops, restaurants and bars, along with a highly sophisticated level of service, but the environment has been left relatively untouched. It's a heady combo of first-world amenities and third-world, undeveloped natural beauty.

A bit like Langkawi itself, if truth be told. One of the pet projects of former prime minister Dr Mahathir Mohamad, Langkawi has good infrastructure, a modern international airport and duty-free status, but a distinctly low-key vibe. The people still drive slowly and high-rises have for the most part been eschewed in favor of low-rise architecture. There is a scattering of resorts along the coastline, and each year Langkawi draws crowds for its Iron Man marathon, but otherwise the island is slow-paced and somnolent. Vast tracts of ancient rainforest still cover its mountainous interior giving succor to numerous tropical birds and animals, and its seas are crystal clear and unpolluted.

Set against a backdrop of towering granite cliffs and rainforest, all parts of the resort are oriented toward the sea. Comprising a series of central pavilions and

pools with 91 spacious villas and rooms scattered within lushly landscaped grounds, it is fairly large. With architecture by Bangkok-based Lek Bunnag and interior and landscape design by Bill Bensley, the resort showcases Islamic art and culture, not just from Malaysia, but worldwide. At the entrance, the lobby tower was designed after a third trip the architect took to the Alhambra in Spain; this is followed by a series of interconnecting pavilions, rough-hewn tall walls and lily pond with an old Malay-style floating pavilion — but no views of the beach. It is only after check-in that visitors continue through a series of courtyards, and become aware of the extent of the site and the stunning sea views. This is quite a clever architectural trick, serving to heighten expectation before all is revealed.

Interiors are no less lavish with each piece of furniture designed with Islamic geometry in mind: the unique idea of the metamorphosis from a circle to a square. The crème-de-la-crème of the accommodation options is the 20 one-bedroom beachfront villas. Each has a staggering 220 sq meters (2,370 sq feet) of living space that includes a private pool garden, patio, spa treatment room with massage beds, huge lounge and bedroom with walk-in closet. Everything is enormous: the spaces, the TVs, the sunken bathtubs (easily big enough for a pool party for four!), the showerheads, the lot. Moorish and Malaysian influences abound: Soaring ceilings, timber floors and soft cottons are combined with the use of pewter grilles, custom-crafted standing lamps, metallic door handles and the like. You almost expect to see a hookah in the corner.

These, actually, are reserved for the Rhu Bar where hanging fabrics, wicker sofas piled high with brightly colored cushions, Chinese Islamic screens and Indian swings give a Middle Eastern atmosphere. This is slightly odd considering you're on an island off the west coast of Malaysia, but hey, the Arabs bought Islam to the region and their traders in dhows used to routinely evade (or not) the local pirates. You can just about get away with this Turkish-delight type milieu when the seascapes — and the cocktails — are so sublime.

Sublime, too, is the over-the-top spa with mainly Asian-inspired therapies, Kids for All Seasons program and a variety of outdoor activities. There is a great library with a wide selection of DVDs, CDs and books, too. Many, however, will chose to head for that lounger — and stay put. They are on holiday, after all.

Jalan Tanjung Rhu, 07000 Langkawi,
Kedah Darul Aman, Malaysia.
tel: +60 4 959 2888   fax: +60 4 959 2889
www.fourseasons.com

The Datai Langkawi

It's always a welcome surprise to find a resort that does more than pay lip service to the environment, so to discover one that is super-sensitive to it is a rare treat. This is the case at the Datai on Langkawi island. It bills itself as a "Retreat to Nature" — and in its setting, use of materials, services and general ambience, it is exactly that.

From the very beginning, the extensive site of 550-million-year-old tropical rainforest dictated the design of the resort. Singapore-based Kerry Hill Architects and local firm Akitek Jururancang used every possible means to impact as little as possible on the natural site. They utilized the existing contours of the land and placed the main complex on a high ridge in the heart of the forest well away from the beach; this kept interference with the waterfront to a minimum. The smaller villa structures and second swimming pool were placed on lower ground to minimize the mass of the main building, and to fit in around existing trees.

The overall result is a resort that is totally attuned with its environment. If you have any interest in the natural world, you'll be bewitched by the sheer diversity on display here. Flying lemurs glide across the night sky from pillar to post; heavy hornbills clamber in branches outside your window; there are wild orchids, sinuous philodendrons and fantastic-shaped ferns. The majesty of the trees is awe-inspiring; the quality of the light and early morning mists ethereal. A dawn or dusk walk with one of the hotel's nature guides is a must; and for those who want something more strenuous, there are mangrove boat trips and longer treks into the interior. For some, simply sitting out and listening to the song of the forest can be enough.

If one views the complex from the sea, it is hardly visible at all. But once you are ensconced within — on the higher level at least — there are fabulous views out to

the Andaman Sea. These are best enjoyed from the 84 rooms and suites housed around the central lobby. Surrounding the main pool, they were outfitted so as to achieve a seamless integration between outside and in. And because all the public pavilions, connected by walkways, paths, bridges and steps, are open-sided, cooling breezes and shafts of light are invited in, as is the surrounding treetop tapestry.

The architecture combines both vernacular influences and Modernist forms. The imposing lobby, an expansive open-beamed structure in *belian* wood with massive shingled roof, is clearly derived from traditional Malay structures, as are the stilted, pavilion-style restaurants, spa and beach house. The accommodation blocks, however, are not. Nonetheless they do not jar, because their roofs have generous overhangs to protect from both sun and rain, and their wooden cantilevered balconies add a rustic touch. Perhaps the most awe-inspiring structure of the whole resort is the tree house-style Thai restaurant, called the Pavilion. Daringly perched atop 14-meter-tall (45-foot) tree trunks, it juts out from the ridge, yet still nestles within the forest canopy. It gives a whole new dimension to al-fresco dining.

The Malay-style villas, sited in a seemingly casual way below the main complex, consist of a wood-enclosed bedroom, luxurious bathroom (almost as big as the bedroom) and a sun deck. Every window, balcony and doorway offers a ringside seat to the arboreal atmosphere. Another option for larger parties is one of the newer pool suites: as the Malay house is amenable to additions, here a series of freestanding rooms similar to the villas are connected to a spacious living/dining area with kitchen, pool and terrace. Then it's only a short walk down a meandering pathway across a gurgling stream to the seaside. A perfect arc of white sand and aquamarine sea, Datai Bay is one of Southeast Asia's most stunning beaches.

Part of the Datai's allure is its ability to cater to different types of holidaymaker. If you are of the lounge-by-the-pool fraternity, with a spa treatment and an afternoon nap your only diversions, the Datai will suit. Alternatively if you want to explore the jungle, play tennis, go mountain biking, diving or sailing, the facilities are to hand. There is a championship 18-hole golf-course in a wonderful rainforest setting — but don't let the giant monitor lizards sunning themselves on the green or the racquet-tailed drongos sweeping and swirling above put you off your stroke.

The Datai is a favorite with celebrities too. During filming of *The King and I*, Jodie Foster and Chow Yun-Fatt took the opportunity to drop everything and take downtime at the Datai. Reportedly they didn't want to leave. Neither will you.

Jalan Teluk Datai, 07000 Pulau Langkawi, Kedah Darul Aman, Malaysia.
tel: +60 4 959 2500   fax: +60 4 959 2600
datai@ghmhotels.com   www.ghmhotels.com

Pangkor Laut Resort Pulau Pangkor Laut

The ceaseless sound of crashing waves, fine white sand, tall tropical trees, the aroma of sensuous massage oils, fluffy clouds in a blue sky, a daytime moon, a sea iguana sunning his plump scaly body on a rock, a family of otters gamboling in the sea … these are only a few snapshot impressions a guest may register from the verandah of his over-water bungalow at Pangkor Laut Resort. Add to that the beauty of the Malay-inspired bungalow itself, the view over the Straits of Malacca to primary rainforest on opposite Pulau Pangkor, the satisfaction of rested muscles post-massage — and you begin to get a picture of this nature-rich resort.

It's a place removed from time and space — literally. With its own 122-hectare (300-acre) island, 80 percent of which has been left as it was found, no TV, no cars and only a handful of other guests for company, it is a place of deep peace. You don't hear kids crying, music blaring or car engines running. And, because it is far enough away from international airports and busy towns, and is a bit of a schlep to get to (unless you use the resort helipad), it is truly exclusive. There is something about staying on one's own private island, after all.

Built in stages over the past decade or so, Pangkor Laut Resort is divided into three separate sections with three distinctly different offerings. The original resort around Royal Bay is a collection of over-water bungalows in wood and some garden and hillside villas clustered round a collection of wooden pavilions and a central pool. A couple of restaurants, a gym, a shop and some semi-manicured gardens, along with a beach fronting a jetty, complete this section. The rooms have been recently renovated, and are comfy with batiks, wood and bamboo flourishes, along with wood-shingle roofs. Popular with both European and Asian guests, it has long been a favored retreat.

In 1996, the hotel group started work on a collection of private estates on the other side of the island *(see page 117)*. Here, nine sumptuous residences, four on the beach, five on the ridge within the embrace of virgin rainforest, may be rented for a three-night minimum stay. Designed to offer a civilized and super-private respite from the outside world, each has a butler, chef and housekeeper, as well as the use of a luxury yacht. Naturally this is the domain of presidents, politicos and publicity-shy celebs (Joan Collins raved about her honeymoon there in 2002), but the Estates open their tranquil doors to anyone who has the time, money and inclination to stay.

The most recent addition is the Spa Villas and Village, an innovative concept that combines luxury and the natural world with health and pampering. Twenty-two over-water villas, built from dark wood in the style of a traditional Malay fishing village, have private verandahs and restful interiors that are an opulent mix of hand-spun cottons, wooden detailing, local craftsmanship and supremely comfy beds. Of note are the massive terrazzo tubs with ocean view and rain shower concealed beneath a slatted wood ceiling. Fruity toiletries, incense cones, citronella insect repellent and bowls of pot-pourri — along with sea eagles outside your window — ensure that Nature's bounty is part and parcel of the package.

The natural world — be it in the crepe ginger or herb garden, hot and cold tubs and pools, fish in reflecting ponds, waves on the shore, or herby steamers and oils — is central to the spa too. With a jungle backdrop and an ocean view, it is sublime. Cosy nap gazebos (semi-open Zen dens for lounging), open beachside pavilions, a *jamu* bar, reflexology path, a 50-meter (164-foot) lap pool and loungers all front pristine palm-fringed Coral Bay. Ayurvedic, Chinese and Malay doctors are on hand — and pan-Asian therapies restore, rejuvenate and bring you back to center.

In addition to this three-in-one concept, Pangkor Laut has a number of different eating and drinking holes, a resident naturalist and jungle trails, as well as a quiet beach at dramatic Emerald Bay. This horseshoe-shaped cove was the submarine pick-up and drop-off point for British army agents during the Japanese occupation of Malaya in World War II; looking at its whisper-quiet, white-sand environs and gently lapping waves, it's hard to imagine it was once a venue for life-and-death liaisons. Now, thankfully, it's more likely to host a sun worshipper than an undercover agent.

The beauty of the island prompted Luciano Pavarotti to declare it "a paradise" in 1994. "The island truly moves me," he told a journalist at the resort's opening. Today's guests — judging by the resort's high occupancy rates — agree with him.

Pangkor Laut Island, 32200 Lumut, Perak, Malaysia.
tel: +60 5 699 1100   fax: +60 5 699 1200
travelcentre@ytlhotels.com.my   www.pangkorlautresort.com

Tiger Rock Pulau Pangkor

When David Wilkinson was an eleven-year-old boy exploring the jungle terrain of Pulau Pangkor, I am sure he wouldn't have envisaged that one day he would own a hotel there. Certainly his association with the island went back a few years (his family always took their annual vacation there) — but a hotel? Never.

The story of Tiger Rock really began one day in the mid 1960s when David was foraging around the area of the slightly decrepit old Dutch fort. That year he had received a present — a camera — and that day he made a discovery. He came upon a large granite boulder amongst the vegetation bearing the cryptic inscription "1743 I.F.CRALO" and the initials "VOC" standing for the Veerenigde Oostindische Compagnie, or the Dutch East India Company. It was a find indeed. More intriguing, it also bore the image of a tiger.

Curiosity piqued, he snapped some photos, and later carefully pasted them into his album. The album was a gift from his grandparents who had owned a house on Pulau Pangkor in the early 1920s. His grandfather knew the place well and explained to his grandson that a child had disappeared near that rock. It was presumed he had been taken by a tiger — and care was needed in the forest around. However, the picture of the tiger was not that of any ordinary tiger, he said: rather it was a beast that symbolized something greater, something the boy may understand when he grew up.

The information was filed away, along with the photographs, and over time the image of the tiger faded. So, too, did the photos. But if you were to take a look at David Wilkinson's boyhood album today — you'd still see the rock, the forest and the fort. But added to them are some newer photographs: There is a Malay-style *kampong* house, a pool and pool house, and a cluster of estate-style hill houses, all set in the forest behind the fort. They look like they've always been there.

In actual fact, they date from the mid 1990s and were built by that self-same boy, third-generation planter David Wilkinson and his artist wife Rebecca. Originally envisaged as a family holiday home, the property now serves as an intimate resort where the emphasis is on seclusion, service and atmosphere rather than full occupancy. When I visited with my family, we were the only guests. However, as word of mouth spreads, this will alter. Nonetheless, as Tiger Rock only has seven rooms in total, it cannot get over crowded.

Set in 5 hectares (12.5 acres) of virtually untouched rainforest, the resort backs onto the 127-hectare (314-acre) South Pangkor Forest Reserve. It offers a back-to-nature experience, albeit tempered with luxury. Even though you are literally living in the jungle (you are asked to check your shoes for beasties before putting them on), the accommodation is extremely comfortable. You can choose from the open-plan and airy Malay-style house, or a room in the stone-and-brick hill house where

many details take their inspiration from estate houses in Fraser's Hill, the Cameron Highlands and the Genting Highlands. All are personally decorated with artworks and fabrics designed by Rebecca; and each is thoughtfully provided with a palette of paints and a sketchpad.

"The idea was to build with as minimal disturbance to terrain and vegetation as possible," explains David. "And because of the style of architecture and the privacy of the site, we've inadvertently created the feel of an era 30 to 40 years ago." The property evokes the rural idyll that the Wilkinsons themselves experienced as children on holiday; this, doubtless, goes some way toward explaining why it has such an established air.

One aspect of Tiger Rock that definitely doesn't hark back to times past is the standard of the service. This is because the resort is in the competent and caring hands of Mohan Kasi, who along with wife Bavani, is central to the Tiger Rock experience. Mohan is enormously welcoming and efficient, and has the uncanny knack of anticipating guests' needs extremely accurately. One morning after a good half hour of swimming lengths in the infinity-edge, jungle-fringed pool, I came up for air ... to see an ice-cool lime juice placed thoughtfully at the pool's edge. Perfect! And later that day, a special feast was prepared for New Year's Eve: not only was the food spectacular, but presents had been bought for the children and sparklers and party hats were provided on a specially decorated table placed poolside.

Such highly tailored, personalized service far exceeds the norm at even a five- or six-star resort. It reminded me of the type of pampering I used to receive from my grandmother when I was a child. Similarly spoiled by Mohan and Bavani, my family was made to feel very special. It hardly comes as a surprise to discover that repeat guests make up a large proportion of Tiger Rock's clientele. I, for one, plan to return.

WD2 Pangkor, Pangkor Island, Perak DR, 32300 Malaysia.
tel: +60 5 685 4154   fax: +60 5 685 4157
email: rebecca@tigerrock.info   www.tigerrock.info

Eastern & Oriental Express Train

There is something undeniably romantic about train travel, especially when you are in a luxuriously appointed private compartment, with your own special carriage attendant who appears at the press of a bell. "Please tell me what time you want your tea," he says with a smile. "I won't knock on the door, as many of our guests have a nap after lunch." Beautifully dressed in *ikat* weave Nehru collar jacket and smart pants, he is as impeccably attired as the train itself.

For this is no ordinary train. It is the Eastern & Oriental Express, a veritable institution in the train world. Complete with comfy "bedrooms" (albeit none with a double bed), en suite shower rooms, bars including one with a resident pianist, library, restaurant cars and observation car, it has a staff of 40. Each week it travels the tracks between Singapore and Bangkok — and is nearly always fully booked. The two-night, three-day journey takes you through the oil and rubber plantations of Malaysia stopping at such historic spots as Kuala Lumpur and Butterworth (where guests alight for a whirlwind tour of historic Georgetown in Penang), through the narrow gorge at Bukit Berapit, up southern Thailand with a side trip to the Death Railway site, finally arriving at Bangkok on the third day. It is a momentous journey — and can be taken in reverse too.

Even though we may be in the 21st century (and the train certainly has plenty of modern conveniences), the overall atmosphere has more in common with the Victorian era than the present day. Indeed, it brings to mind the joy and fervor of the first great locomotives, and the formality found on such routes as the Orient Express, the Flying Scotsman and the Trans-Siberian Railway. For men, black tie is donned at dinner, and the ladies are encouraged to dress up. Flutes of champagne and cocktail shakers are much in evidence, as are fine wines and cigars. By the

second day, a camaraderie between groups of passengers has been established — a mood that is further enhanced by wonderful meals, entertainment (dancing, fortune tellers and other activities) and shared confidences.

Whether you are a train buff or not, you cannot fail but be impressed. Each compartment — be it with pull-out bunk bed, or of the Pullman variety where two beds are made up side by side — is a noteworthy example of space-saving design. Bedside lamps, fresh flowers and Bulgari toiletries are the small details; polished marquetry paneling, soft carpets and pillows, gleaming brass air-con vents and luggage racks, and enlarged windows form the bigger picture. Even though you are tucked into quite a small space, it never seems cramped. Cosy, rather, as you curl up by the window with a good book, a cup of afternoon tea and cake, all the while being rocked by the train's swaying gait.

The on-board general manager has been with the train ever since its inaugural journey in September 1993 — and clearly loves all half a kilometer of its British racing green and beige form. Many of his staff have also been with him since the beginning, so they are well versed in the in-board code of conduct. Silver service at lunch and dinner is so much more civilized when on the move; the chilled white wine in the monogrammed ice bucket with starched white cloth somehow teases the palate more than on terra firma. And if you have food preferences, they can easily be accommodated. Indeed, service matches that found in a five-star hotel.

In fact, the train is actually a hotel on wheels: It has all the conveniences of a hotel, but the added attractions of a movable feast. Each "room" is different; each excursion a new taste of the exotic. As if that were not enough, in 2004 the operator added a new Thai Explorer itinerary: this two-night journey goes from Bangkok to Chiang Mai and back. It allows guests to see some of the ancient Siamese sights in comfort: there's afternoon tea on a classical rice barge in the ancient capital at Auyuthaya, a walking tour of Chiang Mai, a horse-drawn carriage ride in Lampang and a cruise on the River Kwai. And naturally, whilst ensconced in your private quarters, the views of Thailand's rice-paddy and mountain landscape are sublime.

Take a tip: in my opinion, the top spot is the open-air observation carriage at the rear of the train. Here you can feel the wind in your hair, savor the scents of the tropical air, wave at the kids on the side of the tracks — and watch the fireflies come out as night falls over the jungle. After a delicious dinner, it is the perfect place for a nightcap before you turn in.

Singapore Office: 100 Beach Road, #32–01/03 Shaw Tower, Singapore 189702.
tel: +65 6392 3500   fax: +65 6392 3600
email: oereservations.singapore@orient-express.com   www.orient-express.com

Hotel 1929 Singapore

"A hotel is no longer just a place to stay when you are in a foreign country," says Peng Loh, owner of Hotel 1929 in Singapore. "Rather it comes complete with a whole design, branding, lifestyle element." When he goes abroad, he says, he searches for design-conscious, different places to stay: the day when a utilitarian box sufficed is long past.

He is not alone — if the growth of the privately owned, niche boutique hotel is anything to go by. In Singapore, the market has been slower to respond to this trend than other destinations, but with the opening of the funky Hotel 1929 (dubbed "Singapore's first ever hip hotel") — and others following hot on its heels — all that is changing. Judging by the reaction to Hotel 1929 by both clients and press, Peng Loh is simply articulating, and realizing, a global need.

Situated in the heart of Chinatown behind a newly restored row-house façade *(see right)*, the hotel is an intriguing combination of the historical and the modern, the retro and the new. Offering 32 rooms all with en suite bathrooms, they range in size from tiny to small. But the lack of space is more than made up for by the lashings of style. The main focus is on the owner's collection of vintage chairs: with over 100 pieces, there is the Eames' Lounge Chair Metal, Arne Jacobson's Egg Chair, Paul Volther's Corona chair, and even a Cone chair with the original upholstery by designer Verner Panton. There are also vintage lights, funky rugs, bold prints, a collection of black-and-white photos depicting old Chinatown, a rooftop Jacuzzi and award-winning restaurant Ember.

Housed in one of Chinatown's most exuberant streets (Keong Saik Street was once the center of Singapore's red light district), the area has somehow missed the specious restoration undertaken in many old shophouse neighborhoods. Rather, it

Collection of John Renddel Courtesy of National Archives Singapore

remains full of character today: a stroll down it reveals a hodge-podge of traditional coffee shops, surviving tradesman's businesses, local shops, small galleries, even some business with the ladies of the night. "When I bought the premises and began work on the hotel," says Loh, "I was very aware of the area's history. I didn't want the hotel to stray too far from the local context, so I worked closely with Singapore's National Heritage Board — hence the gallery of photographs upstairs, and the intimate atmosphere below."

However, it needs to be stressed that this hotel isn't another historical relic. Far from it. Loh, who worked closely with local architect Simon Chua, was keen to give the interiors a sharp edge. This is partly realized through the generous placement of the owner's chair collection, but is furthered by a sensitive eye for detail and quality materials. The lobby's floor-to-ceiling glass windows, mirrors hiding storage cupboards, shag pile rugs, modern wrought iron chandeliers and a striking orange arc lamp from the '60s are eye-catching from both inside and from the street — and explain why it is sometimes mistaken for a furniture showroom. Ember is clean-lined and restful in neutral shades of taupe, cream and brown accentuated with vintage Louis Poulson ceiling lights and a bar counter tiled in brilliant purple mosaic: chef Sebastian Ng's East-meets-West, clean-flavored food is justly celebrated. Be sure to have at least one meal here.

Upstairs, no two rooms are alike. Because of space constrictions, showers and toilets are only separated from the bedrooms by a glass panel, and many have sinks outside the shower cubicle. Each is decorated with Spanish mosaic tiles in cool oceanic shades, and many have a metallic glaze. In the three suites, tubs either sit on adjacent outdoor decks, or are integrated into the room itself. Each room also has its own individual retro chair, bold patterned cushions collected by Loh in Barcelona, Madrid and Paris, and bed runners in bright, bold textiles from Finnish design company Marimekko.

Hotel 1929 takes its name from the year in which it was built. Having served variously as a brothel, a hotel, a collection of shops with residences above, even a barber's shop on the corner (apt then that a barber's chair sits in the lobby), it is now a thriving small hotel. Clients will be pleased to hear that in 2006 lawyer-turned-hotelier Loh plans to open a sister hotel down the road: called the Majestic, it will feature 30 or so big rooms, a cantilevered pool on the roof, and more of Loh's inimitable style. Watch out for it.

50 Keong Saik Road, Singapore 089154.
tel: +65 6347 1929   fax: +65 6327 1929
www.hotel1929.com

Le Meridien Changi Village Hotel Singapore

For those familiar with Singapore, and more especially with Changi Village, images that spring to mind are of a sleepy backwater with sailing, golf, local food stalls and a slightly time warp feeling. Old colonial bungalows line leafy streets, bumboats ply the waters to nearby Pulau Ubin and casuarina trees line the beachfront. It's the place that Singaporeans go for a semi-rural break: you couldn't be further from downtown, geographically and in terms of architecture and atmosphere, if you tried.

It's surprising then to find a distinctly trendy, upscale, urban hotel in such a setting. And more surprising to find that it works — really works. From its eye-catching, clean exterior *(see left)* to its up-to-the-minute interior, facilities and service, the Changi Village hotel epitomizes sleek, modern hoteliering.

An enormous amount of thought and planning went into the concept of the hotel. "It is a bit like a chameleon," explains project manager Chng Kiong Huat, "because the hotel can change itself to meet the needs of different customers." Certainly, state-of-the-art business facilities attract companies looking for off-site planning sessions; the spa, pool, and leisure facilities (golf, tennis on request, trips to Pulau Ubin and beach) are great for weekenders wanting a retreat from the city; and extensive banqueting facilities are good for larger parties and weddings. In addition, the hotel is very close to the airport so it's perfect for people with a one-night stopover in Singapore.

If you fall into the latter category, once you've checked in you'll be ruing the fact that you have to leave the next day. The intriguing exterior sports a white-and-glass façade punctured with neon-colored laminated glass balconies. At night it looks particularly stunning as the glass is back-lit and the balconies glow like so many fluorescent pink, green and blue suspended boxes. And once through the hotel's sliding glass doors, the interior has more surprises. A series of open-plan, multi-functional spaces is revealed — pared down yet tactile. The clean lobby opens out into a wine bar and lounge, which is itself semi-separated from the main restaurant. This has huge floor-to-ceiling glass windows with panoramic views over Changi's golf course. Close by are a series of lounges that double up as closed or open meeting rooms.

The ambience within is high-tech modern; the view without, a tropical panorama of forest, ocean and beach. Ambient sounds keep the tempo lively in the lounge, while upstairs on the rooftop a cool infinity-edge pool surrounded by a lava stone and timber deck and planter boxes with grasses and frangipani give a resort vibe. There is a casual, quiet mid-level courtyard where giant tree ferns and a koi pond offer a peaceful spot for contemplation; but if you head into the basement, function rooms are business-like and boardroom busy. The hotel certainly has the ability to reinvent itself for different events and customers.

This is contributed in large part by the choice of materials: five-star marble and luxe velvet have been eschewed in favor of tough Silestone (a type of artificial stone that gives a quartz surface), laminated table tops, clean bleached oak, glass in a variety of forms, and boxy PVC furniture. Automobile paint is used for metallic effects, and Axminster carpets in earthy, khaki tones are luxurious underfoot. No expense has been spared on the lighting: be it the cute cut-glass numbers on the reception desks, the lobby's circular hanging lamps or silk Morning Glory standing lamps, they are usually spot on. Similarly, trendy Swarovski crystal door handles, niche decorations and signage are up-market modern. Painstakingly planned and executed with an emphasis on quality finishing, these choice elements are more than eye candy. They elevate the hotel admirably.

In keeping with the clean ethos of both setting and service, the hotel steers clear of excess ornamentation. Rather, some of the details become artworks in themselves: veneered and lacquered bamboo headboards offer ample decoration in the rooms; stacked glass is used to eye-catching effect on the bar counter, a panel by the open-plan lifts and on a central lobby sculpture; and a crystal, red flower and swirling lightbox arrangement guides the eye in the restaurant.

For such a multi-purpose hotel to truly work, it needs to be very flexible. Staff need to multi-task, the different outlets need to communicate and the element of surprise has to be maintained. Forced to open in mid May 2004, a little earlier than planned because a local gentleman had organized his wedding there — the hotel is proving up to the task. As a spokesperson noted of the wedding party: "The groom is a local customer, he knew what he wanted, and we delivered." All credit to them, I say.

The Changi Village Hotel is a first for Singapore. It's an international hotel, on the one hand open to the wider arena and, on the other, anchored to its immediate environment. A bit like a global village really. It's an ambitious concept that, so far, seems to be working.

1 Netheravon Road, Singapore 508502.
tel: +65 6379 7111   fax: +65 6545 0112
www.changivillage.com.sg

Raffles Hotel Singapore

It could be argued that Singapore's Raffles Hotel shouldn't be in this book. It is full of history and glamor, legendary, opulent, chic even ... but cool or hip? Surely not. It opened in 1887 for a start. It is named after the long dead founder of colonial Singapore — hardly politically correct in this day and age. Half the hotel is given over to a shopping arcade. Virtually every visitor to Singapore tramps through its public spaces to take a photo of its façade or sample a Singapore Sling in the Long Bar. These are hardly the required ingredients of a hot hotel experience.

Nevertheless, a recent stay at the hotel managed to convince me otherwise. There is something undeniably romantic about pulling up on the elliptical gravel drive (preferably in a taxi from one of the hotel's fleet of burgundy-colored London cabs) and being welcomed by an imposing Sikh doorman. Then, when you are ushered into the Carrara marble atrium lobby where antiques gleam under light thrown down from a central glass clerestory, dignified members of staff stand to attention. I had been expecting the architecture and ambience to feel old and sad, but in actuality it was modern, elegant and imbued with life.

It's difficult to pinpoint, but dare I say it, the red-carpet welcome makes you feel a little bit special. Once in the lobby, you're escorted up the sweeping dark timber staircase ahead and you enter what Somerset Maugham called the symbol for "all the fables of the Exotic East." Marked "Residents Only," you can't help but feel a bit exclusive, even a tad smug.

With only 103 suites scattered in five wings around courts, verandahs and lawns, this feeling of exclusivity lingers with you during your stay. You can easily shut out the public areas: A walk in the private expanse of the Palm Court where original Livistona palms and Plumeria trees give shade is tranquil and cool. A cup of tea in one of the main building's spacious drawing rooms is civilized and quiet. Service is warm and efficient. The rooftop pool is a cool oasis of seclusion and the spa a perfumed haven. After a while you come to realize that old-world opulence can be very enticing.

You also realize that the private hotel part reserved for residents (yes you're a resident at Raffles, not a guest) is quite small. This is in keeping with the original concept, as the Sarkies brothers threw open Raffles' doors in 1887 with only ten rooms — and allowed the hotel to grow organically from there. In its glory days, Raffles hosted many a distinguished visitor to the Far East in what was really quite an intimate setting. Today, it honors those writers and dignitaries with special suites named after them; the Somerset Maugham Suite, with personalized letters from the writer and photos of him in residence, is of particular note. Elsewhere black-and-white photos of glamorous dinner dances adorn corridor walls — and before you know it, you're imagining how the lobby looked when the band struck up, or how

the Tiffin Room tables groaned under the weight of a New Year's Eve banquet, even how the poor tiger looked beneath the billiard table.

This sense of history (and myth) is an integral aspect of the Raffles experience. A photo of Ava Gardner who stayed at the hotel in the 1950s exudes high-life, Hollywood glamor; a pre-dinner drink in the Writer's Bar brings to mind Conrad and Coward, cocktails and colonialism, a heady mix if ever there was one. Stories of the hotel's legendary hospitality are to be found at every turn: Rudyard Kipling was a great admirer, as was James Michener who remarked "to be young and have a room at Raffles was life at its best."

I understood what he was getting at (OK, maybe not the young bit!) as I luxuriated on my private terrace overlooking a vista of lawn and lush planting. Suites are as commodious — and coveted — as a Birkin bag. And like a Birkin bag, they are an accomplished mix of traditional craftsmanship and modern élan: antiques, silver, historical china and period prints sit side by side with all the amenities you expect in a modern hotel. From the hardwood floors and priceless Persian rugs to the exceptionally high ceilings (4.3 meters/14 feet) and cavernous interiors, they bring to mind images of the hotel's heyday. Yet they are practically designed too: Reading lights are very good; the TV is large; magazines are thoughtfully provided; and round-the-clock butler service is excellent.

Designated a National Monument in the late '80s and meticulously restored before its grand reopening in 1991, Raffles is also a fine example of how modern-day Singapore celebrates its past, yet looks firmly to the future. Lee Kuan Yew once famously noted that Singapore wasn't ashamed of its colonial history. Taking note, Singaporeans have embraced the old hotel's latest incarnation and, once again, it sits at the heart of the city-state's social scene. A celebratory dinner at the Grill, a game of billiards in the Bar or a performance at the sweet Jubilee Theatre are all highly recommended.

But I suggest going one step further: Check in for the full shebang.

1 Beach Road, Singapore 189673.
tel: +65 6337 1886   fax: +65 6339 7650
www.raffleshotel.com

The Fullerton Singapore

From the seamless check-in to the friendly service in the Executive Club, world-class cuisine and understated almost minimalist rooms, a stay at the Fullerton Hotel flows as smoothly as the Singapore River that runs beside it. Colonial conversions on such a grand scale can sometimes lose direction, but this hotel manages to balance a prestigious historical legacy with a thoroughly contemporary feel. You are aware of the grandeur especially when you're in the open-to-the-sky, glass-roofed lobby — but it stops short of being overwhelming.

Formerly housing the General Post Office on the lower floors and, at various times of its history, the Chamber of Commerce, the Singapore Club and the Inland Revenue Authority on its upper floors, the 1928 Fullerton Building was a Palladian gem. With its fluted Doric colonnades and lofty portico, the imposing building was a fitting testament to the power and splendor of Empire. Then, as now, its situation dominated the waterfront. On one side were the harbor and warehouses that fuelled the fires of trade, on the other Raffles Place, the center of commerce. Today, it is a landmark on the harbor and extremely well positioned for the Central Business District.

In large part because of its position, the building was earmarked for conservation at the turn of the century, but a use had to be found for it. The answer came in the mid '90s when property developers Sino Land Company and Far East Organization acquired it, spent S$400 million and three years on its restoration — then reincarnated it as a prime hotel on January 1, 2001. It hasn't looked back.

Even though it primarily caters to the business traveler market, the Fullerton is by no means just another executive hotel. Certainly its convenient location, broadband internet access in all 400 rooms, digital video-conferencing facilities and so on are a boon — but business-like doesn't mean boring. There's a full range of

leisure facilities including a spa and infinity-edge swimming pool with views over the river, as well as a number of quality eating and watering holes. The Fullerton also plays a central role in the social and business life of the city-state's residents.

Take the Post Bar, for example. With its high tables, back-lit marble tables and ambient sounds, it has become a bit of a hub for the trendy crowd, who often pile in to imbibe cocktails in the early hours of the morning. Local culinary maestro Tung Lok Group runs the prestigious Jade restaurant: here modern Chinese cuisine is served in opulent surrounds. For a more casual atmosphere, there is riverside dining at Town or a snack in the central Courtyard, a good meeting place amongst boxed bamboos and intimate seating nooks. However, the crème-de-la-crème of entertaining experiences has to be had on the roof. Here the hotel can organize an intimate reception in the former lighthouse glass-house, where nighttime harbor views, fine wine and food are a heady mix 36 meters (120 feet) above street level.

When booking, request a room with a view over the harbor and the wonderful durian-domed Esplanade arts complex. When I stayed in an eighth-floor executive corner suite, floor-to-ceiling glass windows offered a cinematic view of bumboats and tugs chugging to and from nearby Clifford Pier, and to skyline and ocean beyond. The ever-changing panorama was an entertainment in itself.

Suites are simple and uncluttered. Limited edition photos of the Silk Route by local publisher magnate Hans Hoffer complement the neutral tones of carefully chosen

fabrics and furniture. Beige, taupe and cream comprise the color palette — soothing and comfortable on the eye. Two sets of curtains, one for night and a gauze one for daytime, are electronically operable, should the light streaming in from across the harbor prove too harsh. Attention to detail is evidenced by a free shoe-shining service and a portable step exercise machine. It, however, remained beneath the bathroom cabinet for the duration of my stay!

Restoration projects are a tricky affair. As well as paying attention to quality physical conservation, they need to retain the spirit and ambience of a building. Often too much attention to the former can lead to neglect of the latter. "When we set out to restore the Fullerton Building, a historical edifice so inextricably linked to the Singapore story," says Philip Ng of Far East Organization, "our task was to preserve the dignity and character of the original building. At the same time, we wanted to create a deluxe hotel that is technologically advanced to meet 21st century needs."

Treading the fine line wasn't easy and it didn't come cheap — but the end result is a grand hotel that straddles past, present and future with an easy authority. Bravo.

1 Fullerton Square, Singapore 049178.
tel: +65 6733 8388   fax: +65 6735 8388
reservations@fullertonhotel.com   www.fullertonhotel.com

The Scarlet Singapore

Like a box of chocolates, full of "naughty but nice" confections, a stay at the Scarlet is all indulgence. From its glitzy lobby to its Swank, Passion and Lavish suites amongst others, not to mention gloriously decadent "ordinary" rooms, this hotel is plush, neo-boho and bold. With its distinctly adult ethos, it is a welcome addition to Singapore's hotel scene. Indeed, it could be argued that the arrival of this bordello-style boutique hotel is representative of the city-state's wider coming of age.

Better known in the past for its "can nots" rather than its "cans," in recent years Singapore has been letting its hair down a bit. Strangely enough, the local media felt this was official when dancing on bar tops became legal, but in our view the design boom and the influx of funky bars, clubs, restaurants and such luminaries as the sexy Scarlet are far more telling. They signify an individualistic bent, where creativity, entrepreneurship and real talent have been given full rein. Full marks, we say.

Owned and operated by newcomers Grace International, the Scarlet bills itself as "vivacious, uninhibited, bold and sensuous." Situated in a series of renovated row-houses and an adjoining Art Deco building *(see left)* in Chinatown, it combines history (think louche, lounging mandarins in opium dens) with something very "now." Behind the trad façade, with its row of ground-floor retail outlets, lies a thoroughly modern operation. Hip eateries, designer chic bars, a pavilion on the roof, up-to-the-minute technology, trendy staff uniforms, and an interior design that is part Rococo, part opulent Oriental, part tropical deco: these are all part of the package. Rooted in history? Yes ... but totally modern, nonetheless.

Modern minimalist, however, the Scarlet is not. There's a signature scarlet palette, a hefty dose of gilt and gold, metallic and black — colors and combos

more at home on a risqué lingerie set than an interior decorating scheme. This is completely intentional, I might add. Forget the monochromatic Nineties, the hotel says. Rather, embrace lush textures, old-fashioned glamor, tassels and swags, plump pillows and pretty pictures. Lounge in a sea of cushions, sip a cocktail, don those stilettos. Dine in splendor. There's nothing wrong with lavishing attention on yourself — and your partner — after all.

The Scarlet offers 84 rooms including five individually themed suites along with three restaurants and bars with suitably saucy names. Even though some of the rooms are small, all are boudoir-chic à la Vivienne Westwood. Many have sweet, lantern-lit balconies and all feature marble-clad bathrooms or shower rooms. In-room amenities include complimentary broadband internet access, cable TV, mini-bar, daily cocktails and nibbles as well as super-sensual toiletries. Suites are larger and decidedly sumptuous: Each is different with subtle wallpaper, custom-crafted furniture including gorgeous bed headboards and the funkiest chairs you can imagine, plus loads of velvet cushions, even a chaise longue and a cocktail cabinet in one or two. Corridors in the hotel have state-of-the-art lighting behind custom-designed metal grilles and doorbells on leather pads. Attention to detail is exemplary.

The public spaces are no less well executed. Mosaic fountains on each side of the main entrance flank the double-height lobby, where a freeform upper floor

balustrade vies for attention with a glorious central chandelier. On one side is the dark and inviting Bold bar — recommended for intimate encounters. Desire is a white and bright pillared dining room that doubles up as a multi-media light show in the evenings; here the menu features a selection of starters ("foreplay"), a number of "quickies" (set lunches) and more heavy-on-the-innuendo dishes. For tropical dining, try Breeze on the roof: This is more of an outdoor Mediterranean-style terrace bar and restaurant. In addition, the Scarlet has an outdoor Jacuzzi, full-scale gym (called Flaunt) and a boardroom, although I can't see much work being done here!

With a portfolio of properties under redevelopment in Singapore, the Scarlet is the group's flagship — and the first to open its doors. (There are other more standard hotels already operating, but they are to receive makeovers too.) Executive director, Geeson Lawadinata, explains that the group thinks not in terms of the cost, but in terms of the results. He is aiming for something totally new in the hospitality sector in Singapore — and certainly the Scarlet is groundbreaking in its milieu.

Giving interior design company Indez a firm brief and a healthy budget seems to have paid off. Our suggestion? Go and check it out. We're sure you'll just lurve it.

33 Erskine Road, Singapore 069333.
tel: +65 6511 3333   fax: +65 6511 3303
www.thescarlethotel.com

The Sentosa Resort & Spa Singapore

Sitting al-fresco on a tropical evening looking through the silhouette of trees out to sea … idly counting the twinkling lights on the horizon (albeit from tankers, but at night you can't see that!); sipping a glass of kir, sampling delicious grilled seafood; watching one of the cooks in the open-plan kitchen deftly plating up. Listening to light jazz. The South China Sea stretching out into the inky black night.

This is the experience offered at the Cliff, the superbly designed outdoor evening restaurant at the Sentosa Spa & Resort. All is chilled, everything flows. After all Sentosa translates from the Bahasa as "tranquility." It is difficult to believe that downtown Singapore, Southeast Asia's high-tech, high-rise, bustling epicenter, is a mere 10-minute car journey away. For the atmosphere at the Cliff is more country than town, the feeling is of a resort rather than a metropolitan hotel. You are in the city, yet it feels like you're in the jungle.

The same can be said for the island of Sentosa itself. Situated just south of the Central Business District and attached to Singapore by a causeway, it has retained a green, fresh outlook, both physically and in essence. Much of the island has been left as it was found. Giant ficus, kapok and *pulai* trees with magnificent sturdy trunks still offer shelter to long-tailed macaques, a variety of birds and other wildlife. Other areas house golf courses, walking and cycling trails, a butterfly park and a vibrant beach life — all outdoor attractions that encourage the visitor to interact with the natural world. It's a great away day for Singapore's residents and tourists alike.

Nestled within 11 hectares (27 acres) of this untroubled terrain, astride a cliff and amidst wonderful landscaped gardens is the Sentosa Resort & Spa. Designed more than a decade ago by Kerry Hill Architects with interiors by the famed Ed Tuttle, the hotel represents a milestone in resort architecture. Finally, a low-rise hotel with over

200 rooms — neither busy and bustling, nor noisy and crowded — had been built. Furthermore, even when it was full, it seemed timeless and relaxed.

The emphasis was, and still is, unashamedly natural. Reflecting lily and lotus pools, low-rise architecture, carp ponds, a 35-meter (115-foot) midnight-blue-tiled swimming pool, tennis courts and an extensive garden spa keep guests in tune with their tropical surroundings. Fan-tailed peacocks stroll around, there's a 3-km and a 6-km (1.8- and 3.7-mile) jogging track, a short walk brings you to the beach, and most of the public spaces echo the type of indoor-outdoor architecture popularized by Geoffrey Bawa in the 1970s and '80s. The hotel is entirely suited to the tropics.

The open-plan ethos allows for framed views from various parts of the resort. Take the centrally sited Pavilion bar, for example. An open-sided structure, it has cool marble floors, colonial-style rattan furniture and pots of white orchids — as well as vistas over the swimming pool on one side and across reflecting ponds on the other. Through breezes alleviate the need for air-conditioning, while a grand piano and jazz crooner create the perfect backdrop for sundowners. It was here that pop-star guest Robbie Williams gave an impromptu post-concert recital in 2003 – and broke the hotel's sound system! Undeterred, he continued singing without a microphone.

He certainly wasn't the first high-profile guest to enjoy the hotel's relaxed, laid-back charm, but, when pressed, staff proved tight-lipped about its celeb clientele. Their privacy is paramount, they insisted. Quite right too, I felt. But take it from me,

many a showman has graced its suites and villas, valuing the exclusivity and privacy the resort offers. Incentive and business groups also find the Sentosa amenable: the conference rooms are flexible enough to cater for events with 20 or 400 participants, and many a couple has tied the knot here. The extensive grounds and numerous outdoor spaces are perfect for wedding receptions.

Another highlight is the individual two-bedroom pool villas, which are nearly always taken — so be sure to book well in advance. Private and discreet, with small gardens and spacious rooms, they are great for birthday celebrations and the like. Other rooms and suites are tastefully decked out in tones of jade, green and sage with liberal splashes of burl wood. All have high-speed internet access, TVs, DVD players, as well as minibar and the like. Many a stressed Singaporean has simply driven across the causeway, checked in for the night, taken time out in the spa, dined in splendor at the Cliff — then returned to the city the next day rejuvenated and refreshed.

The Sentosa Resort & Spa gained entry to the Small Luxury Hotels of the World in 2004, a tribute to its excellent facilities and understated elegance. Is it the perfect "get away from it all" destination, but with metropolitan amenities to hand? You bet.

2 Bukit Manis Road, Sentosa, Singapore 099891.
tel: +65 6275 0331   fax: +65 6275 0228
www.thesentosa.com

Valley Wing at the Shangri-La Singapore

The Shangri-La chain is one of Asia's premier hotel groups. The flagship Singapore hotel has an A-list clientele as long as its lobby *(see right)*. Known for the opulence of its interior décor and commitment to high-quality service, the Shang (as regulars call it) is probably best known for its wonderful garden. With 15 acres and over 110 varieties of 133,000 plants, it is a seminal example of how landscape and architecture can be combined successfully in a tropical setting. Referred to locally as "Singapore's other Botanic Gardens," there is no other hotel in the city center with such exotic and spacious grounds.

When the owners decided to refurnish and upgrade the hotel's super-exclusive Valley Wing in 2003, it was to the garden that the interior design firm gravitated. "The heart of the hotel is its garden," says Charles Robertson of LRF Designers, the firm contracted to oversee the renovation, "and everything else percolates out from it." Bearing this in mind, he restructured the lobby, meeting rooms and breakfast room to make full use of garden views, and built an al-fresco terrace overlooking the central swathe of green. Furthermore, the Valley Wing grand entrance was substantially improved, and guests staying in the three specialty suites were given private lifts and access.

Clearly these suites are the preferred address for visiting heads of state, royalty and captains of industry (the Presidential Suite has housed both George Bush and Donald Rumsfeld amongst others), but for "ordinary" guests, a stay in the standard rooms is anything but standard. The Valley Wing experience begins with a complimentary transfer from the airport, then a friendly check-in at the Champagne Bar adjacent the lobby. One thing that is immediately apparent is highly personalized service (members of staff here are exceptionally good at recognizing faces and repeat guests are treated as friends) and the excellent complimentary "extras": breakfast in the morning, free laundry and dry cleaning, cocktails and canapés in the evening, wine and champagne all day and a 6pm checkout if required.

The renovation process, explains Robertson, was "evolutionary not revolutionary," so as not to alienate regular Shangri-La guests. The hotel wanted to retain its signature style — extravagant East meets classic West — but execute it in a more contemporary manner. So deluxe rooms and suites retain some features (a neutral butterscotch palette, lattice wood panels flanking the windows, period furniture), but have been imbued with updated technology and new accents. Desks have a panel on the top with broadband connection, power point and fax socket (something close to my heart as I seem to spend inordinate amounts of time scrambling beneath desks searching for plugs) and the in-room safe with power socket is large enough to house a laptop. An Asian-style wooden trellising separates the bedroom from the bathroom where deep tubs with obligatory LCD screen, large showers and

innovative, two-level lighting options (bright and functional or mood-oriented) are spacious and inviting. Amenities in the room include custom-made Burmese-style boxes housing leaf tea, coffee and cups, an iron and ironing board in a cupboard, super high-quality damask throws on the bed, a Queen Ann-style chair and signature chandelier. It's a case of having the practicalities, but casting them within a veneer of refinement and beauty.

Specially commissioned artworks flow seamlessly from suites and rooms to public spaces, and beautiful paintings are even incorporated into a panel in the lifts. In the lobby, white marble, a double-height ceiling, priceless art, full-height glazing and a rich, warm palette of soft furnishings combine with garden views and light to create a plush space. State-of-the-art lighting ensures different moods at different times of the day, and if it is early evening a harpist is on hand. There's a warm, residential ambience — and because there are only 136 rooms in total, an intimate guest experience is ensured.

The Valley Wing is really a hotel within a hotel: For the swimming pool and other food and beverage outlets, guests need to venture to one of the other wings. But quite frankly, with 24-hour room service, breakfast room and champagne bar, a private butler on call, personalized pillowcases, bathrobes and stationery sets, absolute privacy and exclusivity — why leave? Robertson sums it up: "The Valley Wing is all about fine luxury, understated elegance and class, with a touch of Oriental grace."

It has the ambience and facilities you expect in the West, levels of service Asia is famed for and touches of culture anchoring it in the East. It is opulent, but never ostentatious. Put it like this: if you want to impress someone, take him or her to the Valley Wing.

Orange Grove Road, Singapore 258350.
tel: +65 6737 3644   fax: +65 6737 3257, 6733 1029
sls@shangri-la.com   www.shangri-la.com

The Metropolitan Bangkok

The city of Bangkok, always a creative hub, is now a burgeoning international design destination. Homegrown cottage industries have transformed into global concerns. Cutting-edge art, furniture and product design are catapulting their way into magazines, homes and offices in the West. Big names like Donna Karan and Madonna are buyers; and Thai names like furniture designer Ou Baholyodhin and florist to the stars Sakul Intakul are equally well known in London and New York as they are at home.

This new wave of design talent often relies on traditional Thai-style materials and motifs, but blends them with a modernity and aesthetic culled from the West. Hence the boxy chaise longue crafted from water hyacinth reeds, the cubist noodle bowl in celadon, the Thai silk cushion with bold geometric patterning. These — and a whole lot more — are as likely to be found gracing space in a New York loft as in a Bangkok bijou apartment block.

No surprise then that Como Hotels chose Bangkok for its Asian counterpart to the Metropolitan in London. The design gurus of the hotel world have once again read the prevailing zeitgeist with uncanny crystal ball clarity. Just when Bangkok began to emerge from the Asian crisis with confidence and vision, the Met opened in swanky South Sathorn. The city was crying out for a sleek center for creatives to congregate in. And even though the younger sibling may lack the superlative (Hyde Park) views of its big sister, its interiors more than make up for this shortfall. Combining clean-lined creativity with commercialism, this hotel has panache.

The Metropolitan, Bangkok, bills itself as "a calming haven within the urban sprawl," and this has more than a ring of truth to it. Interior designer Kat Kng has managed to create something that is both new and timeless — a rare feat. Aided

by museum-quality lighting, flexible spaces, high ceilings and plenty of natural light, the interiors of the Metropolitan are pared down and modern, yet comforting and comfortable. A clever combination of Ming-style furniture, whose sober lines work well in 21st century spaces, and custom-crafted *makha* wood consoles ensure the lobby is easy on the eye. Ditto the blue glass and stark white palette in Cy'an, the main restaurant, and fiery red resin and dark wood in the Met Bar. Mac zealots will be pleased to see iBooks and iMacs with wireless computer access throughout.

The pervading mood in the 171 guestrooms, that include one two-bedroom suite and four penthouses with double-height ceilings, is of sequestered ease. Thoughtful touches include a yoga mat and meditation chair as well as excellent reading lights bed side. As befits both location and the hotel's aesthetic, artworks by young Thai talent Natee Utarit feature various interpretations of the lotus. The lotus is revered in Buddhist Thailand as a symbol of purity; here Utarit's compositions imbue both private and public spaces with a special, one may even say sacred, serenity.

There's no doubt that brand-zealous guests will gravitate to the Metropolitan. If they are fans of the original Metropolitan, they'll see hotel uniforms by Yohji Yamamoto (instead of Donna Karan) and a Met Bar that equals its Park Lane counterpart in vibe and vibrance — and will feel right at home. Singaporean yoga aficionados will slip into a Shambhala session — and have their favorite juice at Glow after. Cocoa Island and Parrot Cay sun-seekers will appreciate the familiar Italian-made robes and signature scent of the aromatics in the bathroom, as well as the crisp cotton sheets. Although each new property is a million miles away from the cookie-cutter chain approach and each is bespoke, they all share a kind of East meets West sensibility. It's a somewhat indefinable concept that is directly attributable to the owner — but once you've been to a couple of Como hotels, you'll get it. And desire it elsewhere.

If, for some reason, you don't get to stay at the Met, be sure to eat there. The talented Australian chef Amanda Gale is a dab-hand at coaxing sensational flavors from simple, fresh produce: be it the Moorish or Mediterranean dishes in Cy'an or fragrant fusion food at Glow, it's heart-warming fare. It's sustenance for mind, body and spirit — and just the ticket before venturing into the *sois* and streets of brash, brassy Bangkok.

27 South Sathorn Road, Tungmahamek, Sathorn, Bangkok 10120, Thailand.
tel: +66 2 625 3333   fax: +66 2 625 3300
info.bkk@metropolitan.como.bz   www.metropolitan.como.bz

The Sukhothai Bangkok

The Sukhothai, situated in the embassy and commercial district of Bangkok, is a design stalwart. Named after the first of Thailand's old capitals (literally meaning "Dawn of Happiness"), it opened in 1991. Despite its age, it is still an assured combination of understated architecture and opulent interiors, and many frequent Bangkok visitors wouldn't consider staying anywhere else. An elemental fusion of teak, granite, mirrors, ceramics, water and the finest of Thai silks provide them with a restful environment after a day of work, sightseeing or shopping.

Paradoxically, its elegance may have contributed to the hotel's chequered history. Accented as it is with Sukhothai-style art, sculpture and ornamentation, it has always run the risk of being considered too cerebral or too much like an art gallery. Were the hotel with its long corridors and wide courts low on occupancy, it could be deemed a little museum-like. But when I visited, there was a buzz and a bustle about the place that many of the Bangkok-based say has been absent in recent years. When questioned, people in the know said that new management had "breathed new life" into the Sukhothai's voluminous halls — and it was once again poised at the heart of metropolitan life.

For most patrons, the hotel's low-rise serenity is a delight after teeming, increasingly high-rise Bangkok. Designed by Kerry Hill Architects, it consists of a series of interlocking buildings surrounding open-to-the-sky courtyards. None is over nine stories in height. There's an extraordinary tactile feeling throughout — and this is fully realized in the stunning lobby: here columns lined with specially woven silk support a double-height ceiling beneath which sits a tuberose and lotus sculptural arrangement by famed floral designer Sakul Intakul. Ornamental pagodas stand in a reflecting pool behind, and high-rise mirrors accentuate the space. The overall feeling is sensuously minimal — a sensibility that continues through the entire hotel.

The interiors were conceived by Paris-based Ed Tuttle. As the Kingdom of Sukhothai was a golden age of Thai art and civilization, so is the hotel a repository of fine art. Two water courts with lines of ornamental *chedis*, one in brickwork and one in bell-shaped metal, Sukhothai-style statuary and a plethora of terracotta bas-reliefs should be more suited to a temple complex, but in fact fit (more than) fine. It is to the designer's credit that these elements — executed in a style that is over 750 years old — can, and do look, so modern. As do the high-quality, almost obsolete materials — hand-fired glazed ceramic tiles, specially woven silk, rare teakwood and durable granite — utilized in modern forms; custom-designed furniture influenced by traditional styles but conceptualized in up-to-the-minute designs; and museum-worthy artworks placed in unconventional spots. There is no doubt that the interiors look as sensual and strong as they did in the early '90s. How does Tuttle do it, we ask ourselves?

The hotel layout encourages exploration. Intimate corners reveal singular details — a huge temple bell by the bar, a lounging daybed with triangular Thai cushions affording views across a courtyard, a hidden black-tiled shallow pool replete with resting statue, ceramic jars with glossy fan palms. Even the octagonal lift lobby delights: there's a gold leaf effect on the outside of the lift doors and granite and mirrors within. The signage throughout the hotel is rather quirky.

As befits such drama, guest rooms and bathrooms are enormous. Within their cavernous spaces, expect teakwood paneling, stone carvings and Thai silk panels. Colors range from muted rust to iridescent shades of gold, rich greens to deep grey, taupe and silver. Silk upholstery even extends to custom-made teak window panels that can be pulled tight against the morning sun, tissue box holders and kettle cozies. This devotion to decorative detail continues into the teak-and-granite bathroom where his and hers sinks, massive mirrors, over-sized bath, ceramic-tiled shower (some with side jets as well as overhead) combine with cotton robes, slippers and a whole array of toiletries. You could easily be forgiven for eschewing a night on the tiles for a quiet evening in … and prompt room service naturally comes complete with serenity.

The Sukhothai has three restaurants, the fairly recent, monumental La Scala, an Italian food lover's dream; the well-established Celadon (Bangkok residents more often than not chose this Thai restaurant for an authentic Thai feast); and the airy Colonnade that serves international fare and a famed Sunday Brunch. These, as well as the ballroom and gardens, are sought-after venues for parties, book launches and other celebrations.

And because the grounds are extensive, there is space to spare. Mature trees, established plantings, an expansive spa in the planning and a tranquil swimming pool are cool and fragrant. In many ways, spending time at the Sukhothai is like chilling out at a resort. It is a powerful antidote to downtown Bangkok.

13/3 South Sathorn Road, Bangkok 10120, Thailand.
tel: +66 2 287 0222   fax: +66 2 287 4980
info@sukhothai.com   www.sukhothai.com

Aleenta Resort Pranburi

If the concept of transforming dreams into reality sounds, well, unreal … take a trip south of Bangkok past Hua Hin and visit modish boutique resort Aleenta. Translated from Thai, *aleenta* means "a rewarding life"; translated into reality, it's the culmination of one person's dream to create "the type of hotel where I would like to stay myself."

As Bangkok is huge, hot and hectic, Aleenta is small, cool and idyllic. Set on secluded 5-km-long (3-mile) Paknampran Beach, it is little: a dozen rooms only. It is quiet: there's a no-kids, no-TV policy and nothing to do. It is restful: the sounds of the surf, ocean views, a plentiful supply of well-thumbed paperbacks and magazines and a tranquil spa provide the only diversions. If you're a stressed-out exec or a couple who need some two-time without the children, Aleenta is for you. It is sophisticated enough for today's global traveler, but it is also beguilingly simple.

The owner and creative force behind Aleenta is Anchalika Kijkanakorn. Today she is an international traveler and businesswoman, but as a child she spent numerous holidays at the family villa just a stone's throw up the beach from Aleenta. "I always loved this place," she reminisced, "so it was only natural when I grew up to buy a plot of land and build a hotel here." After buying the land, she enlisted the help of her brother and architect Pantharat Intarapim — and within 18 months Aleenta was born.

Sometimes, less really can be more. Aleenta's beachfront site is compact, but what space there is has been used imaginatively. A number of white rendered concrete structures are clustered in a garden setting; with stucco covered walls, they exude a part Mediterranean, part rustic *casa mexicana* feel. Thatch and bamboo roofs, irregular shapes and heights and a mix of planes, voids and curves somehow all work together. Three of the freestanding villa rooms appear African-inspired: thatch topped and almost totally circular in shape, they're a sophisticated play on

a tribal form. Other buildings sport upstairs terraces, rounded French windows, bamboo pergolas and decorative tiling. Flagstone-and-pebble paths interconnect all areas of the resort.

On arrival, you enter a small reception area that reveals itself as the resort's biggest building. Magazines and flowers are scattered on a circular sofa, and soft, scented towels soothe away travel fatigue. Upstairs is a curved bar, open-air restaurant and small mosaic-tiled pool *(see right)* with views over the ocean. It's a dazzling sight looking out to sea from the pool's edge, but for really vertiginous 360-degree views, go one level up to the Sky Spa. Here, you see mountains behind, a sublime seascape in front — and swarms of dragonflies around. Like a secret eerie, the circular domed space comprises one open-plan room; it's a scented bower of beauty, with the heady aroma of aromatic oils hanging in the cross breezes.

Even though the setting is Thai, the increasingly clichéd Thai-style is noticeably absent. A few Lanna pots are giveaways, as are the silk runners and cushions, but for the most part the atmosphere is more Greek isle than Gulf of Siam. Hammocks sway somnolently on seashore decks, while tiny-tiled azure pools gurgle and bubble. Every room has its own character: all have sea views of some nature and en suite slate-lined bathrooms, and many have little private plunge pools, but none are the same. All rooms encourage you to open blinds, shutters and French doors to give salty sea breezes access, but you have the alternative of air-con of course.

The restaurant and room service menus are seafood-oriented, and perfectly tasty, though absolutely not haute cuisine. Ditto the staff: dressed in soft white cottons, they are gentle, smiling and eager to please. This makes a refreshing change from the robotic routines you often find in big-city hotels. With the exception of higher management, all are hired locally, and trained in situ. At Aleenta, you feel they want to learn, want you to enjoy the tranquility of the place, and care about you.

Since it opened, Aleenta has created quite a stir. Lauded in both the local and international press as Thailand's "first boutique hotel," it is being careful not to let the accolades go to its head. There is a homeliness to both staff and hotel that the owner and manager are determined to retain. However, they're forward-looking too. Guest chefs from Tuscany, yoga retreats with famous yoga practitioners and Aleenta's very own CD of smooth, classy lounge tunes are some of the newer additions to the Aleenta experience. Those, along with a barefoot walk along an isolated beach, should be enough to be getting along with.

183 Moo 4, Paknampran, Pranburi, Prachuabkirikhan 77220, Thailand.
tel: +66 32 570 194   fax: +66 32 570 220
gm@aleenta.com   www.aleenta.com

Napasai Koh Samui

From Australia to America, Italy to Iceland, people now recognize the name of Koh Samui. What was once a laid-back, coconut grove and rice paddy emerald isle is now a bustling tourist destination with hundreds of hotels and homestays. When the first tourist came in 1971, it was a case of a sleeping bag on the beach. White sands, sapphire-blue sea, a few local farmers and fish-and-coconut cuisine characterized a stay there. Now, the beaches are packed with places to stay, as well as shops, bars and nightclubs — and the population has mushroomed. Between July and November 2004, 200 high-end new hotel rooms opened! There are busy roads, a golf course, and an airport as well as the ferry port at Nathon.

If all this sounds a bit too much, don't be put off. Some quieter areas remain, especially in the south, and the interior hills of granite and limestone are still covered with dense forest. Many of the island's inhabitants, both incomers and the original fisher folk, are friendly and warm; and walks to waterfalls, fishing, snorkeling and diving trips, elephant riding and mountain biking take you away from the crowds. If it's peace and quiet you're after though, you need a hotel away from the action.

The Napasai on Ban Tai beach at the western tip of Maenam is one such location. As soon as you turn into the driveway, everything slows down — and you can breathe again. It isn't miles off the beaten track or anything; it just has an all-pervading restful civility about it. Fronting a calm bay with palm-fringed beach, it is set in a cashew grove with views over the nearby island of Koh Phangan and gorgeous sunset vistas.

Originally owned by French company Pansea Hotels & Resorts that has now merged with Orient-Express Hotels, the resort has a distinctly Gallic air. Indeed, much of its clientele comes from continental Europe. I happened to stay during the weekend of their grand opening party, where the hotel's owners, press and various

Thai and French dignitaries mingled on the lawn for a champagne reception and dinner dance. In his address, the French Ambassador talked lyrically about French-Thai relations, and how the resort epitomized the synergy between the two countries. "The Napasai architecture has wonderful Thai style," he declared, "while there is also a French sensibility as seen in the French cuisine and certain aspects of the hotel."

Francophiles will appreciate hotel literature in French, welcome chocolates in the room, French and German stations on cable TV, the predominantly French music selection, the French-style Ytsara spa, and European management. All contribute to the *je ne said quoi* of the resort. This is echoed in the architecture too: while it is undeniably Thai in concept, it displays a somewhat restrained, European flavor. For example, roofs are elegantly curved, but they lack the sinuosity and flair of traditional central Thai style.

In fact, the architecture can best be described as assured resort style: With a central pavilion-style reception, bar and restaurant, individual villas radiate out on either side of the public spaces. There are 55 cottages, 45 suitable for couples, and 10 larger ones that are great for families. Thai details like Lanna woodcarvings, basketry, traditional *tang* (low seats with lion claw feet used as tables) and Northern Thai runners on the beds anchor the resort with a firm sense of place *(see right)*. As do staff in fisherman's pants and baggy shirts. Nevertheless, the overall feeling is quite European. There are also 14 larger privately owned villas on the periphery of the resort; these are available for rent when the owners are not in residence.

For the sportsman, there is a dive center, canoes and a topper for guests' use, also two tennis courts and priority booking at Samui's nearby golf course. Staff can arrange car hire and boat trips, but many guests choose to chill out by the infinity-edge pool with views out to sea. Somehow, life seems quieter, more restrained and genuinely slower once you enter the resort. The island's multitude of attractions is easily accessible and the airport a mere 15 minutes by car, but inside the Napasai's boundaries you are in a world removed.

Napasai translates from the Thai as "clear, blue sky" and after a morning's shopping at nearby Chaweng or a visit to Big Buddha, a leisurely afternoon poolside makes for a halcyon day. Blue skies reflect in the glittering water and sea, pool and horizon merge into one. Bliss.

65/10 Ban Tai, Maenam, Koh Samui,
Surathani 84330, Thailand.
tel: +66 77 429 200   fax: +66 77 429 201
samui@pansea.com   www.pansea.com

Costa Lanta Koh Lanta

When four childhood friends decided to "do something" with a piece of land on the relatively remote and undeveloped island of Koh Lanta, they didn't have a clue as to how it would turn out. They knew they didn't want "Thai style"; they knew the land itself should be the star and no trees should be felled; and they had a vague interest in the concept of camping in the casuarinas. But that was about as far as it went.

Indeed it had taken quite some time to agree on the idea of having a hotel at all. But once that decision was made, the friends were in total agreement. They simply briefed architect Duangrit Bunnag with all their dislikes about hotels, then gave him a creative free rein. This modus operandi was both brave and novel (as is much of the hotel itself) — but it proved to be remarkably successful.

So much so, that soon after opening, Costa Lanta garnered interest from design mavens, architectural reviewers, and both local and foreign press. The flurry of copy, subsequent entry into the Design Hotels' portfolio (www.designhotels.com) and Honorable Mention Award from the Association of Siamese Architects under Royal Patronage, resulted in the über-cool coming in their droves. Whether they were ad execs from Bangkok or designers from Scandinavia, they had no qualms about the relative obscurity of both site and setting — and gave the hotel the thumbs up.

Certainly, Costa Lanta is a very chilled place. Twenty-two cabins are set in a 26-rai (4-hectare/10-acre) plot of scrub-and-grass, planted with a variety of trees and fronting a casuarina-fringed coast. Connected by boardwalks and a sluggish clay red water body that curves through the site like a ponderous question mark, it has a fashion-forward vibe throughout. Amenities are few: an uncompromising 6-meter (19-foot) high restaurant with lounge upstairs *(see left)*; a linear, dark-tiled pool; a raging, active, roaring sea; and the beauty of a site left as it was found.

Each boxy villa sits on an exposed concrete plinth and is encased within a wooden beamed structure topped by an outer polycarbonate shell and an inner sheet of canvas. Worthy replacements for the Thai-and-tired thatch cottage, each functions modularly. Two sides of the cabin are static and concrete, while the other two comprise two timber "doors" that can be pulled back to open up the interior. Inside, there's a simple mattress on a wooden platform *(see right)*, slate grey exposed concrete walls, floaty mosquito net and a rigorously appointed semi-outdoor shower room.

Materials — stone, recycled wood and concrete — are simple and rugged. Bunnag, who prefers to eschew architectural discussions about style and focus on setting, says they were chosen precisely to blend in with the natural environment. "I love all the trees on the site," he explains, "and I tried to expose them throughout. By structuring all the buildings with a very simple approach, I succeeded in putting all the architectural vocabulary in the sublimity of its context. The high-ceilinged restaurant was designed to provide great views of trees and ocean. In the villas, the canvas roofs and open bathrooms were intended to allow guests to feel they are truly living under the shade of the trees. The idea of the pool is also visual; I tried to make it disappear."

In Bunnag's view, the context is all at Costa Lanta. The architecture is just there to complement it. The owners echo his sentiments: "Design may seem like the paramount aspect of our philosophy," they say, "but it is just the backdrop of what we call life — life in the open. We believe that Costa Lanta is an equation between urban comfort and the desire to escape from it. Each room is a proposition to take another look at what seems evident: a tree, a door, a window." Certainly, when you are sitting on your deck, idly watching a monitor lizard stroking across the river while a heron skims ahead, you understand why. Kingfishers, butterflies and other birdlife are plentiful by day; owls can be seen by night; and every minute brings the roaring sounds of surf through the trees to your door.

The fact that you are sitting in a cutting-edge cubist cabin watching it simply adds to the view. Many agree: repeat guests are the norm at Costa Lanta. Whether these folk are attracted by the inspired choice of music in the lounge, the clever name, the clean Thai flavors in the restaurant, or a combination of the above, they keep coming back for more. In fact, a fashion designer from Europe liked the hotel so much she returned the following year with designs for staff uniforms. That shows commitment, doesn't it?

212 Mu 1, Saladan, Lanta Yai, Krabi, Thailand.
info@costalanta.com   www.costalanta.com

Amanpuri Phuket

Cool hotel aficionados will no doubt have visited Amanpuri, Aman Resorts' first hotel, at some point. If they haven't, they will certainly have heard about it. Over the years, kilometers of copy have been dedicated to it and thousands of guests have enjoyed its tranquil serenity. After all, the resort opened in 1988. Longevity — as well as design, service, comfort, exclusivity — is a parameter that should not be overlooked when judging a hotel. A stylish hotel doesn't necessarily have to be new. It can be old — as long as it is timeless.

This is perhaps the secret of Aman Resorts. Or at least one of their secrets. Many of the older properties (as long as they have been properly maintained) have aged well, and in large part this is due to the timelessness of their design. Utilizing indigenous building styles and materials, keeping rooms simple and placing the hotels in suitably exotic locations are just some of the strategies that ensure many of Aman's resorts don't date.

In addition, Aman Resorts consistently deliver an enlightened service philosophy, private surrounds, high-end facilities, ultra-deluxe comfort, total guest privacy and a low-key, casual atmosphere. Therein lies their success. Targeting the top-end consumer who has more money than time, they reign supreme in their particular niche market. Most Aman *aficionados* wouldn't even consider another brand.

Repeat guests comprise a large percentage of the clientele at Amanpuri. Set in a coconut grove on Phuket's coveted west coast, many come annually for a two- or three-week break. And why not? The resort looks as stunning today as it did when founder, Adrian Zecha, opened it in the late '80s. A rigorous annual maintenance program has seen to that. Yet even in the early days Amanpuri was miles ahead of its competitors. In scale, architecture and atmosphere, it was the exact opposite of the big, brash, 400-room hotels that were so popular at the time. It flew in the face of conventional hoteliering.

Edward Tuttle, the American-born architect and interior designer based in Paris, designed the resort. Taking his inspiration from the temple architecture of Ayutthaya, the old Thai capital, Amanpuri comprises a series of Thai gabled structures — airy pavilions, *salas* and villas — covering 24 hectares (60 acres) of hilly headland. The lobby, restaurant, bar and other public facilities are housed in a cluster of open-sided buildings with multi-tiered Thai-style roofs set around a dark-tiled rectangular swimming pool. From here it is a short walk down a steep flight of steps to a crescent-shaped beach where loungers and a gym are located. The complex is particularly dramatic at night.

Trisara Phuket

With the colonization of the island by planters over 100 years ago, the face of Phuket changed forever. Vast swathes of primary rainforest were torn down and replaced by regimented rows of rubber or coconut trees. After this first wave of commercialism, a second ravaged the forest further. This time miners delved deep underground in search of tin. The third wave occurred a few decades later, and took the form of the tourist dollar. At this point in time, the coastlines bore the brunt of the development: hastily constructed hotels, badly planned tourist centers, loud jet-skis and rows of deckchairs nudged (or bulldozed) traditional fishing villages aside.

It's amazing, really, that the island has survived at all. And doubly amazing that people still visit it. Nevertheless, Phuket thrives — with approximately 4 million estimated tourists visiting each year. Some come for the sun, sand, Singha beer and a healthy dose of *subai subai* (laid-back charm) — and leave two weeks later. Others choose to buy into the building boom that saw 50 new villa developments constructed in 2004. Others have been waiting for Trisara to open.

They need wait no longer. And they won't be disappointed. Far from it. Because not only does this landmark property sit in an area of coastal wilderness that has survived these various commercial onslaughts, it does so with the kind of glamor associated with the grand hotels of the past. From its magnificent Thai-style public buildings to each individual pool villa or villa residence, the resort is imbued with refinement and elegance. Furthermore, it is only a short ten-minute drive from the airport and has the best sunsets on the west coast.

Sounds too good to be true? Well, it isn't. Since it opened in November 2004, it has been praised by press and punters alike — hardly surprisingly when you see its facilities. In addition to bigger and better pools, pavilions and public spaces, each

of the 33 individual freestanding pool villas sports a gargantuan 200 sq meters (2,150 sq feet) of total space, which includes a private 10-meter (33-foot) pool with uninterrupted ocean views, spacious deck and superbly designed interior. The suites are impressive for their space and comfort, rather than over-the-top opulence.

Everything was planned down to the last detail — and doorknob. "We wanted the rooms to be really comfortable," explains general manager Anthony Lark, "After all, how often do you stay in a hotel, and find the chairs are hard or the light switch is too far away from the bed? Our intention here was to iron out all those irritating aspects — and give guests a practical, as well as supremely relaxing, space."

Be that as it may, visually and spatially they are pretty ravishing too. There are choice Thai-style artifacts (a *chofa* on a stand, a Khmer-style statue), black out curtains behind shot-silk drapes, a specially designed chaise-style chair and stool that can double up as a child's bed, a study area with office facilities, and indoor and outdoor bathing options. Air-con is virtually silent, but if guests prefer a fan, the one above the bed has been specially wired to be almost soundless too. Quiet and seclusion are key at Trisara: it's to be commended that each villa is some distance from the next — and because 800 of the site's largest trees were retained, you often cannot even see your neighbors, let alone hear them.

No expense has been spared on the facilities either. For the activity-orientated there are plenty of diversions: tennis (plus hitting partners), golf, a fleet of yachts, a 100-meter (328-foot) swimming pool for laps, diving and shopping are but a few of Trisara's offerings. There is also a library with a wide range of books, magazines and games, plus thousands of hours of music downloadable onto iPods or CDs. For those more horizontally inclined, there is a world-class spa with Asian and Western therapies, plenty of loungers, and the type of peace and privacy found only at truly exclusive destinations.

Because it is set in 21 hectares (52 acres) between two private headlands with its own beach, Trisara has space to spare. Site to guest ratio is huge. And as the resort is cradled in the type of landscape that first covered Phuket — pristine, unmanicured, natural — it has an almost primeval beauty about it. From any of its forested paths you may catch glimpses of a pavilion roof, a blue pool, the odd umbrella — but you have the illusion of being alone. Beneath the canopy, with only vegetation, shoreline, ocean and horizon for company, you're totally private. That is a luxury in today's world.

Nai Thorn Bay, PO Box 6, Thalang 83110, Phuket.
tel: +66 76 313 333   fax: +66 76 311 999
info@trisara.com   www.trisara.com

The Racha near Phuket

The small island of Koh Racha Yai is best known as a day-trip destination. Its four beaches have fine white sand, azure waters stacked with coral and fish, and a quiet environment that is the antithesis of over-developed Phuket. Even though it is only a 25-minute speedboat trip from Phuket's southern tip, it is a million light years away in amenities and atmosphere. After a day of snorkeling, sunning and swimming, you'll be loath to leave its beguiling shores.

Luckily, as from 2004, you don't need to catch the last boat home. This is because Sanctuary Resorts opened a new boutique hotel, appropriately called the Racha, on the island. Check in, and after the last day-tripper has gone, you have the island to yourself.

This is not strictly true (as there are some backpackers' huts and a few beach restaurants scattered here and there), but it may as well be. With the dusk creeps a stealthy serenity: the only sounds are the lapping of the waves on the shore, the odd peacock squawk, maybe some ambient music from hidden speakers on the deck. It's a perfect Thai isle night in the middle of the Andaman Sea — and your only companions are the lapping of waves and a bright swathe of stars above.

Set over 8 hectares (20 acres) in the embrace of horseshoe-shaped Bay Ba Tok (West Bay), the Racha offers design-conscious villas with all the facilities today's disposable-income traveler has come to expect. There's a PADI dive center, holistic spa, wireless internet access in the main block, star-gazing terrace with state-of-the-art telescopes on the roof, innovative cuisine, a full-entertainment system with satellite TV in the rooms, Jacuzzi baths, some private plunge pools — and more. The more comes in the form of the secluded luxury of the natural environment.

Sanctuary resorts has the lofty aim of creating sustainable tourism projects that benefit the local infrastructure, both socially and environmentally. On the social front, they are working with the seasonal Thai workers who come to the island to sell drinks, umbrellas and loungers and snorkeling gear to day-trippers. They are keen these folks keep their jobs; in fact, they actively support them. But because local populations are tiny, the main aim at the Racha is environmental. The company is trying to obtain protected marine status for the bays and surrounding coral reefs, and the hotel helps with education about anchor practice and over-fishing. The resort also encourages marine researchers to come and share their knowledge with both guests and local residents. On a more prosaic level, the hotel has a sound waste disposal system, room keys that activate electricity (so guests can't leave lights and air-conditioning on when they are absent) and a fervent commitment to recycling practices.

Sanctuary also believes that a holiday should be about balancing mind, body and spirit. Of course this may be achieved simply by chilling on the seashore, but

for those who want a bit more, a number of Masters in Residence programs are offered. Here, healing, yoga and other experts run a variety of workshops on an ad-hoc basis. The best way to check out what is running where is to visit the website. Believe me, it's a refreshing change from the clichéd beach barbecue.

Also refreshing is the fact that the resort is the antithesis of the over-used, and frankly rather tired, teak-and-tile Thai style. This is not to say that Thai style doesn't have a place in Thailand — of course it does. But with a totally new property, it's fun to see a modish architectural milieu where influences are more Tandao Ando than temple-inspired. Conceptualized by M L Sudavdee Kriengkrai, before this commission better known for her interior design projects, the resort is chic and minimalist. The low-rise, yet monolithic, main building, with rooftop 35-meter (115-foot) infinity-edge pool is unashamedly international. There is no thatch (rather the roofs are of bitumen tiles) and the only coconut wood you're likely to see is growing outside your front door. Materials are exposed concrete, rugged grey stone quarried on the island, rendered concrete and creamy terrazzo. The only concession to tropical style is the reflecting pools and some sweet river pebbles and slatted wooden mats in the bathrooms.

The all-white villas feature clean, cool interiors, a decent-sized terrace with a small modernist *sala* to one side, cavernous indoor-outdoor bathroom and the usual amenities. Some have private plunge pools. Polished white cement floors and bed stand and bedside tables fashioned from concrete keep things cool. Alleviating the starkness is some clean-lined furniture made from organics. Funky rattan chairs, coconut-wood lamps with hessian shades, water hyacinth weave on the desk chair, and natural cottons on the daybeds keep you grounded to the environment.

Because the environment is really what the Racha is all about. A Robinson Crusoe idyll — but with all amenities included. Can't be bad, eh?

Koh Racha Yai, Near Phuket, Thailand.
tel: +66 76 263 688   fax: +66 76 264 023
reservation@theracha.com   www.sanctuaryresorts.com

Mom Tri's Villa Royale Phuket

There is an innate grace in things Thai. You see it in the palms pressed together greeting, the lowering of the eyes, the gentle smile. The soaring teak bargeboards of traditional temple architecture. The delicate carving of fruit and vegetables. The sound of a child's voice.

Grace is evident — in droves — at Mom Tri's Villa Royale, an exclusive boutique hotel on the island of Phuket. Set on a promontory between Kata and Kata Noi beaches in a verdant garden setting that tumbles down a steep cliff to rocks and the Andaman Sea below, it comprises only 18 suites. Formerly one of the homes of owner-architect Mom Luang Tri Devakul, it pays homage to his love of Thailand's art and architecture. From the moment you enter the luxuriant secluded garden estate, your holiday experience is suffused with age-old Thai serenity.

The hotel appeals to people who shy away from staying in hotels. It has the air of an informal house party: guests are encouraged to borrow from the extensive library, linger in front of the owner's collections of art and artifacts, or drop into the high-ceilinged gallery where changing exhibitions are held. Drinks are served on an open-air verandah bar, or beneath the shade of an old sea almond tree. Meals ditto: Mom Tri's Kitchen is well known for its flexibility, as well as its rightful reputation for stocking the freshest of ingredients and there's an extensive wine cellar. Paths meander through the ornamental gardens, and you're invited to wander at will.

Glorious Thai architecture and craftsmanship are exhibited at every turn. A clearing reveals an enormous Lanna temple gable, a niche an old spirit house with fresh offerings. Ceramic tiles from Lampang are inset into walkways, a wooden balustrade of an intricately carved *naga* hangs from a corridor wall, and sculptures of sinuous figures by the owner shelter beneath trees. A serpentine path leads past the saltwater swimming pool literally crafted out of seaside boulders *(see left)*, past the newer freshwater pool, and down to adjacent Kata Noi beach. Gracious staff members, in soft white shirts and baggy pants, ensure you secure a lounger, towel and cool drink once you are sea-side. Indeed, they'll look after your every need during your stay.

Over the years, the hotel has grown organically in a number of different ways. The initial thatched roof pavilion where Mom Tri lived and entertained (today's bar) gradually expanded over time. Other buildings, including the main dwelling with its steeply pitched roofs and high wooden ceilings followed, and the reception area, gallery and shop were added. In the same way, the garden has evolved and grown in. Originally planted by Mom Tri with the help of landscape designer/writer William Warren using indigenous plants as much as possible to create a screen against the strong salty monsoon winds, it has been reworked several times. More recently, German landscaper Reimund Reisinger has contributed to the lush, varied planting.

Similarly, the decision to open the home, initially as a restaurant, then as a six-suite hotel, and finally in its present form, grew from circumstance rather than design.

As befits its idiosyncratic history, guest accommodation is scattered around the site, and many of the suites are different. Where they are united, however, is in their elegant Thai proportions. All are spacious, and furnished with sumptuous silks, opium-mat bamboo wall panels, superb gold leaf decoration, Persian rugs and paintings on wood that are mainly adaptations of temple murals from Wat Pumin in Nan Province. In the newer block, some of the rooms have deep ceramic outdoor tubs, as well as breathtaking views through trees and foliage over the ocean. The end Pool Suite has a small plunge pool and sexy outdoor shower overlooking Kata Noi beach. From every vantage, the sound of the waves crashing on the rocks below, running water, the breeze in the trees and shafts of Asian sunlight reinforce the feeling of languorous tropicality.

In the last couple of decades, Phuket has become associated with large hotel developments and a newer, brasher sensibility. Package tourists have gradually replaced the individual traveler, and many claim that Patong is the new Pattaya. Villa Royale acts as a reminder of the island's early days — when the beaches were quiet and clean, the traffic was minimal and much of the island was accessible only by boat. As the hotel's slightly old-fashioned name suggests, Villa Royale offers a return to graceful living in private surrounds where the age-old Thai traditions of hospitality are honored.

The guest directory warning "in spite of the good will of the staff and of our efforts in English language training, some understanding problems may occur" is really not necessary. In fact, the standard of English is very high. That notwithstanding, a warm, receptive heart is often more comprehensible than words — and this is a given at Villa Royale.

Kata Beach, Phuket 83100, Thailand.
tel: +66 76 330 015–7   fax: +66 76 330 561
info@boathousephuket.com   www.boathousephuket.com

Twinpalms Phuket

Twinpalms Phuket declares on its website that it is "privately owned, passionately run" — and this seems a fair summary. Add to that "photographically ravishing," "perfectly formed," and "perpetually sunny," and you get a bigger picture. For the full frame, take a trip to Surin's casuarina-lined beachfront, turn up the narrow road back from the beach, and visit the resort itself.

You won't be disappointed. First views of the magnificent lobby — thoroughly modern, yet with more than a passing reference to the traditional Thai *sala* — are breathtaking. Slightly raised to provide a visual connection to the sea, it is a glorious, voluminous structure with a very tranquil air. Cool, hip and cutting-edge, it gives a taste of what is to come. At its center is a large timber screen: This acts as a focal point, but delineates space on either side for a wine bar, reflecting pool and restaurant on right and a library *(see right)* and spa on left. It also heightens expectation as to what lies beyond.

This takes the form of a monochromatic lounge area with free wireless internet access (*de rigeur* if you want to be on top of things nowadays) and access to the heart of the hotel. This comprises a central 50-meter (160-foot) swimming pool, accommodation blocks, a freeform lagoon and *sala* — all in a gorgeous garden setting. "The whole project was conceived taking into consideration the relationship between architecture and landscape," explains architect Martin Palleros of Perth-based Tierra Design. "We wanted something suitable to contemporary living, but with some elements of traditional Thai forms."

The latter are subtle and understated, because the main impression is slick, strong and linear. Glass, clean-lined furniture and an almost urban aesthetic predominate. The palm-lined pool has one straight edge, lined with cabana-like twin sunbathing beds with white canopies and sexy metal loungers, while the other side is freeform and curvy. It's a cool open panoramic space, sort of Miami meets the Med. You couldn't be further from the general '70s Phuket vibe if you tried. Thankfully.

Circling this central "spine" are several two-story buildings housing 72 bedrooms and four suites. These are differentiated by size and amenities, but all are united in a design that integrates the rooms with the landscape. Bathrooms have a full-height glass window that overlooks a private garden court, while out front balconies or terraces extend the rooms into the garden. All corner rooms and 40 grand deluxe rooms have striking mock-wooden pivoting louvered screens (actually made from a wood composite for ease of maintenance). "The screens give the occupants a private space while still allowing a visual connection with the surrounding landscape," explains Palleros. Certainly, once ensconced in your refined and relaxed room with the screens closed, it's cosy yet cool.

The general manager describes the hotel as "a must see, must feel modern boutique spa resort that offers affordable luxury," and this is an apt description. What it fails to mention though is that Twinpalms has been conceptualized and executed in a way that is both forward-thinking and fun. Take the evening wine room scenario, for example: On the dot of 6pm, everything you indulge in — wines, cheeses and chocolates — costs $1 per minute. So, set the clock, imbibe, and have a bit of a laugh. Similarly, because the hotel is set some 175 meters (575 feet) back from the sea, if you are feeling lazy, a little *tuk-tuk* ferries you down to the beach club on Surin beach. In-room high-speed internet access is a given, as are the serious martinis, cocktails and brilliant buzz of Oriental Spoon, the hotel restaurant. Other light-hearted touches include access from some room terraces straight into the lagoon pool.

Similarly, detail in both architecture and interior design is exemplary. Strong green glass screens in the bar can be slid open or kept closed to afford privacy, and in the Japanese area of Oriental Spoon, woven screens and water hyacinth furniture add an organic element. Custom-crafted furniture is mixed with such items as tables made from Thai rain drums on the balconies and antique timber chairs in the lobby. Organic elements are incorporated within the hardscapes with an eye for detail — and rotating artworks in the public spaces are chosen with care.

In keeping with the resort's aim to keep abreast of current trends, the Palm Spa is worth a mention. Here, wellness is treated as an holistic concept, so mind/body/spirit modalities are offered, along with the more conventional scrubs and rubs. There is also a decent sized gym.

Be it a spa weekend, a gourmet challenge, a bit of r & r, a lazy sun 'n' sand sojourn, a party — or a combination of the above — Twinpalms caters to all. And the best bit? It's in an environment that stimulates the senses. How cool is that?

106/46 Moo 3, Surin Beach Road, Cherng Talay, Talang, Phuket 83110, Thailand.
tel: +66 76 316 500   fax: +66 76 316 599
book@twinpalms-phuket.com   www.twinpalms-phuket.com

The Rachamankha Chiang Mai

For over 700 years, Chiang Mai has been the matriarch of the kingdom of Lanna, the area where the broad plains of the Chao Phaya River and its tributaries give way to the hills — and for much of its history an independent political and social identity from southern Siam. King Mangrai, the founder of the Lanna Kingdom, carefully chose its site in a broad valley of the Ping River in 1296. Over the ensuing centuries, Chiang Mai grew into the spiritual and artistic center of the north, giving succor and shelter to thousands of sons and daughters. It became an architectural treasure house, and today houses over 300 *wats* (monasteries) — and 500,000 inhabitants.

Increasingly, it also houses a host of high-rises, the result of decades of rapid, unregulated development. Many tower over monasteries, and some even demand the destruction of the city's architectural heritage. Pollution in the form of traffic congestion, noise and waste in the river is also growing. It's encouraging, therefore, to see that not all developments are following this on-and-up pattern. Once such is the Rachamankha hotel which opened in mid 2004.

With the same owners as Tamarind Village, a more economical compact city-center property that has garnered rave reviews and repeat guests in their droves, the Rachamankha is more upscale than its little sister. Yet its roots lie in the same premise that prompted its owners to build the Tamarind Village. Call them diehard traditionalists, but they believe that if Chiang Mai is to survive, it needs less modern construction and more conservation. To this end, both low-rise hotels are high on historical authenticity and atmosphere — and in the case of the Rachamankha, high on style too.

The Rachamankha's main architectural influence is the highly individualistic *viharn* (preaching hall) of Wat Phra That Lampang Luang in Lampang Province, but there are Chinese influences in the layout and interiors as well. Comprising three earthen brick-laid courtyards, low-rise, colonnaded buildings and a central pavilion-style lounge, the hotel adheres to *feng shui* principles. The basic construction is of earthen bricks covered with white limestone plaster, while walls thrust out in the ancient manner and traditional tiled roofs are multi-tiered. Set in a walled compound, the Rachamankha's architecture enables guests to really experience — see, feel and touch — genuine Lanna culture. This was the owners' primary aim.

Because of the construction methods used, the whole complex is serene, cool, secluded — almost monastic in ambience. Where it isn't monastic, however, is in the service and amenities: there's a gorgeous 20-meter (65-foot) swimming pool, a lofty restaurant with paintings depicting the Lord Buddha's life, sober Ming-style

chairs and large Lanna lanterns serving extremely tasty Thai (and fusion) cuisine *(see right)*, an adjacent bar, massage on demand and very attentive staff. And even though rooms are simple, these are no monks' quarters. With 18 superior and four deluxe rooms as well as one two-bedroom suite, each is different. Furnished with one-off antiques scoured from the region, bamboo blinds, Burmese art and Chinese porcelain lamps, they are accessed through an antique Lanna door with ornate handle and wooden bolts.

Other notable features are a library with internet access, a gallery showcasing some of the Lanna Kingdom's finest art and antiquities, a red-pillared pavilion lounge and peaceful gardens. Even though you are within the old walled city a stone's throw from Wat Phra Singh and a 15 minute walk from the Night Bazaar, you'll feel far removed from Chiang Mai's hectic streets. As one guest put it: "As soon as you enter the Rachamankha, you leave the city behind. It is in the city, but not of the city."

It needs to be stressed that none of this has been achieved by cutting corners. The 1.2 million baht investment by the architect/owners is a sizeable sum by any calculation — and each and every detail has been carefully planned. In the same way that Tamarind Village was a labor of love, the Rachamankha is as much about emotion as it is about bricks and mortar. The intelligent nurturing in the construction stages is now fully evidenced in the elegant finished product.

Up until 2004, Chiang Mai had art, architecture, religious sites, cultural tourism, cooking schools, a thriving arts and craft scene and wonderful shopping — but no hotel that truly represented this amazing Lanna treasure trove. The opening of the Rachamankha has filled that gap.

6 Rachamankha 9, T Phra Singh,
Chiang Mai 50200, Thailand.
tel: +66 5341 8892   fax: +66 5341 8893
www.rachamankha9.com

Four Seasons Resort & Spa Chiang Mai

If first impressions are indicative of what's to come, the start of a visit to the Four Seasons Chiang Mai, characterized as it is by sweet scents, cool textures and fragrant tropicality, is nothing short of sensational. Step out of your taxi or hotel limo, enter the soaring high-ceilinged lobby built to mimic the principal structure of a Lanna village *(see left)* … and time suddenly slows down. Significantly. You're ensconced in an elephant *howdah* seat, bedecked with a glorious jasmine garland, all the while wiping your brow with a lemongrass scented icy towel and sipping a tangy pomelo, pineapple and watermelon juice. Ahead are views over a well-established garden, through working rice fields, to the Doi Suthep hills beyond. The breeze brings the scents of exotic flowers and wings of butterflies in equal measure into the open-sided structure.

Thirty km (20 miles) north of Chiang Mai, and you may as well be off the map. The exclusivity of the resort and the privacy it offers are truly relaxing. Even when it's full, you don't have to see anyone. Built in a horseshoe shape around rice fields and a central swimming pool, all amenities are to hand — but somehow you can be separate. There's a fusion of luxury with simplicity, grace with rusticity. The Four Seasons Chiang Mai, I come to realize, is the ultimate hideaway hotel.

The resort has 64 pavilion and 16 residence suites, all raised on stilts. Acharn Chulathat Kitibutr, a prominent Chiang Mai architect who is an enthusiastic proponent of local design traditions and materials, was responsible for the main structures and pavilions. The 16 two-story clusters of four pavilion suites are all teak-built with wood-shingled Lanna-style roofs sporting the distinctive decorative feature at the top of the gable called a *kalae*. Each has its own private gazebo or *sala* and most have hill-and-paddy views. The residence suites, and the more recently built Lanna Spa, were designed by Bangkok-based Lek Bunnag of Bunnag Architects; they are housed in more intricate filigreed wood-and-brick buildings, with oriels, towers and steeply pitched, multi-tiered roofs, giving a magic castle effect. Some have their own private plunge pools, and all have jaw-dropping interiors.

Public buildings — the Sala Mae Rim restaurant, the lobby, library, shop and bar, as well as the pool pavilions — are composed of cream-colored local stone and teak wood. All are set within 8 hectares (20 acres) of landscaped gardens, designed by the Bensley Design Studios in Bangkok. Tropical abundance as a phrase simply doesn't do justice to the profusion and variety of plants here. Heliconias, torch gingers, orchids hanging from tree trunks and countless varieties I didn't recognize constantly attract birds and butterflies. Huge teak trees laden with ferns and climbing philodendrons proffer shade, and there is the ever-present sound of water. A series of walkways, wooden bridges, waterfalls, weirs and streams run through the resort — the latter are designed to irrigate the rice fields and also feed the two lakes.

The resort is more rustic than I had imagined, but of course that is entirely in keeping with its stunning natural location in the Mae Rim Valley. My pavilion suite was accessed via a thunbergia-draped pergola and a set of plain wooden stairs. Going up to the room felt a little like climbing up to a tree house, especially as a mini teak forest with gingers and crinum lilies surrounded it. In fact, relaxing in my open-air *sala* adjacent the room with views over the gardens on one side and the majestic, shaded teak grove on the other was like sitting above my own private arboretum.

Rooms, with interiors by Abacus Design of Bangkok, are a sensuous combination of luxury and homespun charm. The latter comes in the form of lamp shades fashioned from bark fringed with hessian, locally woven curtains, kilim rugs, covers on two water hyacinth chairs in soft local cotton, guest information presented on specially made recycled paper called *sa*, chick blinds — and more. Bed linen is in cool cotton, bathrooms with deep tubs are a study in luxe, and walls of distressed oatmeal have wood-and-gold leaf accents. Televisions are concealed in armoires with bold gold stenciling effect and artifacts reflect the resort's location: a Burmese *hsun-ok* in red lacquer, a locally carved monk figurine on the side table, celadon plates with fresh fruit, and embroidered cushions and runners on the bed.

As befits a Four Seasons property, service is warm and courteous, but it is in the details that the resort excels: there are plenty of hangars, the complimentary bottles of toiletries are huge, the ice is replenished in the pavilions twice daily, there's a well-stocked library. Even though no one else was doing the aerobics class I'd signed up for, I had a personal session with an instructor who obliged with the level I wanted to exercise at. My massage at the Lanna Spa made me feel as if I was walking on air afterwards. The fresh fruit in my room, a bunch of *long kong*, a sort of mix between a longan and a mangosteen, was succulent and at the exact right ripeness. I can still bring to mind its exact perfume. It's this attention to the little things that remain in the memory long after the visit is over.

Mae Rim-Samoeng Old Road, Mae Rim, Chiang Mai 50180, Thailand.
tel: +66 53 298 181   fax: +66 53 298 189
www.fourseasons.com

Acknowledgments

The photographers and author are indebted to many people. Without their help, hospitality and patience, we wouldn't have been able to produce this book. Therefore, we would like to extend a big "thank you" to the following: Jose Luis Calle at the Balé; Guy Neale at Downtown Villas; Hans Jenni, Hansjörg Meier, Tomoka Yamamoto and Jamie Case at GHM; Debbie and Bradley Gardner at Begawan Giri Estate; Maria Kuhn, John O'Sullivan, Putu Indrawati, Liza Quddoos and Royal Rowe at Four Seasons Resorts & Spas; Wendy Kassel, James Low and Trent Munday of Como Hotels and Resorts; Frederic Simon, Richard Daguise and Anita H. Moormann at Alila Hotels & Resorts; Gert Friedrich Kopera and Herminarti Purwanggoro of the Dharmawangsa; Trina Dingler Ebert and Sean Flakelar at Aman Resorts; Ibu Inggrid Meiske and Ibu Anna Bambang Surjo Sunindar of Rumah Sleman; Gabriella Teggia at Losari Coffee Plantation Resort & Spa; Lawrence Loh, Lin Lee Loh-Lim and Rami Nuek of Cheong Fatt Tze Mansion; Adrian Brown of E & O Hotel; Uzma Nawawi and Tracy Khee at YTL Hotels and Properties; Rebecca and David Wilkinson and Mohan Kasi at Tiger Rock; Leesa Lovelace and Myra French at Orient-Express Trains & Cruises; Loh Lik Peng and Mariana Tan of Hotel 1929; Serene Wong Sui Leng, Fong Kah Seng and Chng Kiong Huat of Far East Organization; Robert Logan and Iris Chan at Raffles Hotels & Resorts; Geetha Warrier at the Fullerton; Geeson Lawadinata of Grace International; Yong Han Weelin of the Sentosa Resort & Spa; Annie Tan and Regina Eng at Shangri-La Hotel; Nuchareekorn Kornkirati at the Sukhothai; Anchalika Kijkanakorn of Aleenta Resort; Poonnika Thanasannont and Franz von Merhart at the Napasai; Kasma and Kasira Kantavanich and Karnjana Opaspakornkij of Costa Lanta; Anthony Lark of Trisara; Mom Luang Tri Devakul and Khun Dan at Villa Royale; Nadine Thiemann at the Racha; Olivier Gibaud of Twinpalms; Rooj Changtrakul and Choochart Loha-udom at Rachamankha; Eva Malmstrom Shivdasani, Greg Seddon, Geoffrey Bennun and Warinthon Saena of Six Senses Resorts & Spas; Charles Robertson of LRF Designers, Martin Palleros of Tierra Design, Jaya Ibrahim, Duangrit Bunnag, Antony Liu, Carolyn Ortega, Bill Warren, Chami Jotisalikorn, Nengah and Nova Arnawa, Evelyn Gamueda, Luis Fernandes and Tanis, Max and Kevin McGrath.

First published in 2005 by Periplus Editions
with editorial offices at 130 Joo Seng Road #06-01, Singapore 368357

Photos © 2005 Jacob Termansen, www.termansen.com
Text © 2005 Kim Inglis
Design by The Periplus Design Team
Book grid by Loretta Reilly

Distributed by
North America, Latin America and Europe
Tuttle Publishing, 364 Innovation Drive,
North Clarendon, VT 05759-9436
tel: (802) 773 8930, fax: (802) 773 6993, email: info@tuttlepublishing.com
website: www.tuttlepublishing.com

Japan
Tuttle Publishing, Yaekari Building, 3F
5-4-12 Osaki, Shinagawa-ku, Tokyo 141-0032
tel: (03) 5437 0171, fax: (03) 5437 0755, email: tuttle-sales@gol.com

Asia Pacific
Berkeley Books Pte Ltd
130 Joo Seng Road #06-01/03, Singapore 368357
tel: (65) 6280 1330, fax: (65) 6280 6290, email: inquiries@periplus.com.sg
website: www.periplus.com

10 09 08 07 06 05   6 5 4 3 2 1